Crime-free Housing in the 21st Century

Crime-free Housing in the 21st Century

Barry Poyner

Jill Dando Institute of Crime Science
University College London

Published by

UCL Jill Dando Institute of Crime Science
University College London
Brook House
2–16 Torrington Place
London WC1E 7HN

First published 2006
ISBN 0-9545607-3-6

British Library Cataloguing-in-Publication Data
A catalogue record for this book is available from the British Library

Project management by Deer Park Productions
Design and typeset by Pantek Arts Ltd
Printed and bound by Ashford Colour Press

Contents

Foreword by Ronald V. Clarke

Academics are forever being exhorted to undertake cross-discip-
linary work, but they often meet with indifference or suspicion
when they try to do so. Most of them soon give up the struggle
to gain cooperation or access to the resources they need, and
retreat back to the safety of their own disciplines. This makes it
all the more remarkable that for the past twenty-five years Barry
Poyner, a trained architect, has been engaged on a programme
of criminological research on the relationship between crime
and the built environment. That he has done this successfully as
a private consultant, without any institutional backing, is evidence of his considerable determination.

He brings a unique perspective to this under-researched field. His background in architecture has
given him a detailed understanding of the everyday ways in which people use buildings, and of
the ways in which small changes in design can affect this usage. Without this understanding, he
could never have produced the detailed guidelines for designing out opportunities for crime that
he lays out in this and earlier books. His training has also taught him how to communicate the
essence of these guidelines in illustrations – sketches he has drawn or photographs he has taken
himself. But his training did not teach him that good design could prevent crime. In fact, this idea
was close to heresy, dismissed as 'architectural determinism' by leading architects and criminologists of the day. Instead, he came to the idea as a result of a study of accidental drownings that he
completed at the beginning of the 1980s. When he plotted the drowning locations, he found that
these were concentrated in places with the greatest 'opportunity' for them to occur. For example,
people drowned in canals that were in towns and cities, not way out in the country where few
people ever went. He concluded that in order to obtain the maximum benefit from preventive
measures – such as fences, warning notices and lifebelt stands – these should be focused on the
urban not the country canals. Coincidentally, he noted that road safety engineers had discovered
that many crashes occurred at roundabouts serving as terminals for motorways and, in order to
prevent these crashes, had designed a new kind of junction to connect motorways with existing
roads. With this background of experience, he was open to Oscar Newman's ideas, then just
beginning to cross the Atlantic, about the need for 'defensible space' designs to reduce crime in
public housing.

Newman's ideas greatly influenced social housing policy, but they were panned by social scien-
tists, most of whom thought he had disregarded the social causes of crime. He had played into
their hands by making numerous methodological errors in his research, which was hardly surprising since he had been trained as an architect not as a social scientist. Barry Poyner does not make
these mistakes. Though he may have been trained as an architect, he is by instinct a social scientist. His research is unusually meticulous and its conclusions never go beyond the evidence. Its
particular hallmark, however, is a focus on specific forms of crime. To obtain data on these specific
crime types he and his colleagues – most notably Barry Webb – have often had to sift laboriously
through hundreds of police crime reports to sort them into more specific categories. For example, when commissioned to study 'street attacks' in Birmingham and Coventry, he sorted these
into several distinct sets of incidents – such as handbag snatches, robberies of drunks and pickpocketing at bus queues – each of which depended for their occurrence on clearly defined
situational conditions that provided the opportunity for them to occur. These findings gave him
the raw material to think about ways in which to change the environmental conditions giving rise
to each set of incidents. For example, he proposed different ticketing and queuing systems for
buses which would remove the opportunities for pickpocketing.

He has consistently shown in his work that small changes in design or layout can critically affect opportunities for crime, but that such changes have to be made separately for each type of crime. For example, in this book, which is an updated and much revised version of *Crime Free Housing* that he published with Barry Webb in 1991, he shows that the features that protect cars from being stolen when parked at home are not identical to those that protect the house from burglars. But he goes even further and shows, for example, that design features that deter burglars who want to steal large and bulky items such as TVs might not deter burglars who are satisfied with easily carried items such as cash or jewellery. This is because burglars need a car to transport the former items but not the latter. Certain housing layout and design features can facilitate nearby parking and thus unwittingly help burglars to steal larger items, whereas other features can make such parking difficult or risky for burglars. This degree of specificity is highly unusual in criminological research, but it is absolutely critical if the research is to result in practical crime prevention action.

In fact, it is his determination to make research relevant to practice that drives Barry Poyner's work and gives it the edge of quality. He has never been interested in merely elucidating the relationship between design and crime. Much more important to him has been to ensure that crime prevention design, founded on a solid base of research evidence, becomes an integral part of architectural practice. His ultimate goal is to ensure that architecture plays its proper role in driving down crime. That is why his guidelines are so tangible and practical. It is also why he is a crime scientist and why the Jill Dando Institute of Crime Science is pleased to publish this book.

Ronald V. Clarke
University Professor, Rutgers, The State University of New Jersey
Visiting Professor (2001–2005), Jill Dando Institute of Crime Science

Foreword by Stephen Town

In 1983, I walked my first beat, a crime-ridden and disorderly council estate. Despite numerous arrests, the estate seemed to be dominated by criminals and a small number of individuals whose main source of pleasure seemed to be making life as unpleasant as possible for their neighbours. As a former engineer, I was genuinely shocked at the incredible ease with which so much crime was committed. Houses and cars seemed to have been designed for the convenience of criminals. The housing layout removed any influence and control away from residents. Large grassed areas, lacking any ownership or relationship to people's homes, were abandoned by the law-abiding and had become disfigured eyesores. A network of footpaths and alleyways gave easy access to the rear of houses and helped criminals to wander around the area, searching for vulnerable targets, offending and escaping.

My experience on the streets of Bradford planted the idea that things could be different. In 1995, I became a Crime Prevention Officer in a part of Bradford with one of the highest rates of burglary in the country. One of my first duties was to act as 'advisor' to the Royds Community Association, the resident-led body in charge of a £31 million urban regeneration scheme. The task was a little daunting, but if that idea in my head had any merit, now was the time to act. I began to try to find guidance on housing design and crime. The police had the Secured by Design scheme, but written guidance backed by sound research was hard to find.

Get *Crime Free Housing* was the advice of Calvin Beckford, a Crime Prevention Design Advisor in the Metropolitan Police, but this was out of print. I did, however, manage to contact Barry Poyner who generously supplied me with *Crime Free Housing* and *Design Against Crime*. I quickly added *Design for Inherent Security: Guidance for Non-Residential Buildings* to the list. At last, I was able to study specific guidance on designing out crime in housing that was underpinned by careful research, not the 'vision' or theories of those smitten by the latest utopian dream. Perhaps this is why the recommendations made such sense and tallied so closely with my experience of the real world. As I came to know Barry Poyner I was impressed not only by his willingness to help a policeman 200 miles away, but by his insistence that design should be informed by evidence and research. I later received similar help from Oscar Newman. In time, I would come to see these two men as the giants of my field. They have both shown me considerable kindness, taking the trouble to supply me with copies of their books and invaluable advice.

The title of *Crime Free Housing* was intriguing. The aim was much more ambitious than anything else I had seen, and the importance of design in creating or denying the conditions in which crime could flourish was unambiguously stated. My confidence grew and the result was an increasing influence on the Royds regeneration. Working closely with Les Webb, an architect with a perhaps unique level of informed interest in crime, the scheme has been an outstanding success[1] Using the recommendations in *Crime Free Housing* together with local crime analysis has resulted in a burglary rate of seven times the national average being massively and sustainably reduced. People's quality of life has been transformed, and so has the area's appearance. None of this is meant to suggest that other non-design issues are unimportant – but rather that the potential for design to do huge damage or immense good is massively underestimated. This subject remains a potent untapped source of crime control in this country.

Foreword by Stephen Town

Sadly, Barry Poyner's evidence-based approach to design is extremely rare. I have seen some very bewildered faces when I have asked advocates of a particular layout what evidence they had to support their views. Many of the professionals who should be reading the work of Barry Poyner and Barry Webb are either unaware of it or are more interested in following the latest fashion than in finding out what the latest research shows. One of the greatest indictments of architecture and planning is the fact that it is exceptionally rare for members of either profession to revisit and assess their work. Lessons are not learnt and failure is repeated. Residents and society pay the price and the police pick up the pieces.

New Urbanism is the latest in a long line of fashionable and influential planning theories to emerge and be implemented without any supporting evidence. Worse, in many ways this new fashion flies in the face of the research evidence. According to New Urbanists, for example, access and 'permeability' are not something to treat, as the evidence in this book shows, with great care; they should be maximised. Rear courtyards and rear garden gates that facilitate burglary by providing easy access to the rear of a large number of houses are a consequence of the New Urbanist desire to position houses close to the street and hide cars out of the way. Even the British Crime Survey shows this is a very vulnerable form of parking. Such layouts create problems that will require expensive ongoing management, maintenance and funding – in short, they are unsustainable.

These problems are already beginning to emerge, as this book shows. My own experience is more extreme. The Hulme regeneration in Manchester is described by some as a 'model community' and is widely promoted as an example of New Urbanist thinking. Yet the burglary rate for Hulme for the period 2002–2004 was three and a half times the national average[2].

Crime Free Housing and this updated work demonstrate what could be achieved if we based our designs on evidence. This book is timely and very welcome. I commend it, and the authors' previous work, to architects, planners, designers, developers, police, and all others who care about success, real sustainability and crime-free housing.

Stephen Town
Bradford District Architectural Liaison Officer and co-author of
Design Against Crime: Guidance for the Design of Residential Areas

The opinions expressed here are those of Stephen Town and do not necessarily reflect the views of West Yorkshire Police.

[1] The Royds Regeneration Scheme and its impact on crime is described as a case study in Office of the Deputy Prime Minister/Home Office (2004), *Safer Places: the planning system and crime prevention*. London: HMSO (pages 58 & 59)

[2] In April 2002–March 2003 there were 215 burglary dwellings and a burglary rate of 70 per 1,000 dwellings in Hulme. In 2003/4 there were 208 burglary dwellings and a burglary rate of 68 per 1,000 dwellings. The national rate per 1,000 dwellings for these two years was 20 and 19.8 respectively.

Introduction by Barry Webb

This book shows the extent to which crime in residential environments can be controlled through design and planning. It is much needed. That design and planning can contribute to the control of crime is not new, and there have been other books, theories and official guidance on this topic. The value of this one lies in the strength, scale and detail of the research evidence presented, and the consequent prime role it gives to design in creating self-policing and crime free environments of the future.

Barry Poyner and I published *Crime Free Housing* in 1991. The original research on which that book was based involved a detailed analysis of crime in an area comprising 14,000 dwellings. It remains the largest scientific study so far to have investigated crime and housing layout. For many reasons, *Crime Free Housing* did not get wide attention from planners and designers and is now not easily available. Since 1991, however, the climate has changed with the expansion of house building and planners being encouraged to pay greater attention to crime prevention. There is, therefore, a need now more than ever for easily accessible, high quality and well presented research evidence on crime and housing layout. This update of the original study was therefore commissioned by the Home Office, to whom thanks are due, to make it relevant to the current planning context and more widely available.

One of the drivers for this change in climate comes from the Crime and Disorder Act 1998, which now requires planning authorities, amongst others, to assess the crime risk associated with their policies and decisions. More recent guidance from the Office of the Deputy Prime Minister published in 2004 (after this report was written by the author for the Home Office) urges all those who can influence the design and layout of developments to pay greater attention to crime control. If this is to happen, however, planners and designers need to understand better why they should get involved and the extent to which they can make a difference. This updated version of *Crime Free Housing*, through its detailed analysis of residential crime, provides that insight into why and how design can control crime. It is this problem-oriented focus that is missing in most other guidance, yet it is this that will enable practitioners not only to understand better their role but also to think more creatively and effectively about how to design crime free environments of the future.

From time to time, new forms of housing appear. Experience from the past, in relation to the public sector high-rise apartment block for example, tells us that we need to be much better at assessing the likely crime risk of these new environments before they become widespread. In carrying out this update, the author was able to expand the original study to identify the potential vulnerabilities of the new urbanism style of housing layout. In doing so, he demonstrates the value of a good evidence base on which to draw, and the need to apply principles rather than rigid design recommendations to such risk assessment.

Housing environments are not static but dynamic, continually changing. Often these changes occur incrementally, almost without us noticing. The opportunity to revisit the original study areas 15 years later reveals the extent to which housing layouts and the way residents use them evolve over time. It also highlights the role of design in not only creating but also in sustaining safe communities in the long term – get the basic design right in the first place and crime stays low and may even improve further; get it wrong and it just gets worse.

Introduction by Barry Webb

It is a little unusual to include two forewords to a book. This one, however, has a special significance in that, due to illness, it is likely to be the last major work by Barry Poyner, regarded by many as one of the most significant contributors to this field. It therefore represents a milestone in the field of crime and design research. In inviting Ron Clarke and Stephen Town to reflect on and provide a personal view of Barry's work, I hope it gives a better sense of the impact he has made across the field both academically and in practice.

Barry Webb
Commissioning Editor
Deputy Director, Jill Dando Institute of Crime Science
University College London

Author's Preface

The idea for this report was to update *Crime Free Housing*, to take the original findings of the 1991 publication, review them in the light of subsequent research and to re-present the material in the current climate of planning practice and housing development. Much effort was put into trying to find new research that might have implications for housing layout and crime. In the event, little really new research material could be found and I came to realise just how unique and valuable were the original studies in Harrow and Northampton which led to *Crime Free Housing*. This made it even more surprising that there were so few references to its recommendations in other research and guidance in the field. Whether it was a lack of promotion of *Crime Free Housing*, a lack of interest by the design community, or  a lack of understanding of the findings, it became clear that the research had not had the impact it deserved on design practice. As a consequence, this report re-presents much of the original argument and data, on the assumption that most readers will not be aware of this material.

Recent developments in planning guidance

During this study (2000–2002), there was a considerable amount of government activity revising planning guidance relevant to crime control. In March 2000 the Department of Environment, Transport and the Regions revised and reissued PPG3, the government's *Planning Policy Guidance Note 3: Housing*, followed by its companion guide *Better places to live*, jointly published in the autumn of 2001 by a re-formed Department of Transport, Local Government and Regions (DTLR) and the Commission for Architecture and the Built Environment (CABE). Other quasi governmental guidance also appeared in the housing field, notably the *Urban Design Compendium* produced jointly for English Partnerships and the Housing Corporation published in October 2000. A further important development during the project was the decision by the Office of the Deputy Prime Minister to revise the DOE Circular 5/94 *Planning Out Crime*.[1] The content of this new guidance document was unknown to me at the time of writing.

It is important to appreciate that this report does not attempt to anticipate the outcome of any of these revisions to government policy on planning out crime. The purpose of this report is entirely a scientific one of attempting to summarise what is known about the control of crime through design and layout of housing, and present this material in a form which designers and planners can use whatever the planning context. This has led me to avoid recommending specific solutions to design and layout problems in the way set out in *Crime Free Housing*. The original book listed twelve specific design recommendations (for a summary see Appendix 3 of this report). Here, I have presented the conclusions in terms of evidence-based principles for use in deciding what design strategies to adopt. The idea of this is to encourage housing layout designers to develop and adapt the research findings within the new urban design agenda.

Through-streets and cul-de-sacs

When I began this update project, I knew that one of the most important and sensitive issues would be the question of through-streets versus cul-de-sacs. At the beginning I really had no idea what I would be saying on this in my report. In the work that led to *Crime Free Housing* we had not considered the extent to which these two types of layout were associated with either consis-

1. Subsequently published in 2004 by the ODPM as *Safer Places: the planning system and crime prevention*.

tently low crime or high crime rates. At the time, other design and layout factors seemed more important, for example the provision of footpaths was clearly one issue that affected several crimes in a major way, and the security of access to back gardens was another.

The decision to rework the data analysis for this update, and to try to find a clearer form of presentation, gave me an opportunity to include through-streets, grid patterns and cul-de-sacs in the analysis. The results show that claiming cul-de-sacs are not good for crime control is clearly nonsense. However, the revised analysis shows that cul-de-sacs, like through-streets, are not always crime free and that it is the mix of other layout features that is important rather than the form of street layout. This again led me away from recommending specific design solutions to propose that designers and planners should focus on developing crime-specific strategies for avoiding each of the four principal crime groups (burglary, car crime, theft from around the home and criminal damage). The idea is based on the conclusion that a residential area becomes safe because it has designed into it a core set of key features that make the area unrewarding to potential criminals. This core strategy does not have to contain every recommendation that has ever been made for designing out crime, but it has to be a coherent set of features that work together to achieve the crime-free status. Thus it seems possible that this core of layout features could vary from project to project, allowing designers freedom to develop a strategy that might be unique to their project but based on the findings and principles set out in this report. If this idea of developing different strategies for individual projects is successful it could lead to future opportunities for research on residential developments with new thinking that will create an even more diverse range of possibilities for achieving a rich, attractive and secure environment in which to live.

Evidence rather than theory: but some new theory emerging

Much of the field of designing out crime is packed with theories, from defensible space and territoriality through rational choice and routine activity theories to environmental criminology. All of them have their value but they are not made a focus of in this report. The intention of the original study was to present evidence of how design and layout influence the presence of crime in residential areas to convince the design community that relatively crime-free environments ought to be achievable. This unashamedly atheoretical approach continues here.

Although this update is not primarily concerned with developing theory, there are two issues that have arisen suggesting theoretical developments may emerge from this work. First, it is possible to claim much more for design than before. In *Crime Free Housing* the claim was merely that design was an important option in the armoury of crime prevention strategies and so planners, designers and developers had a responsibility to contribute to this important area of crime control. Now, with the experience summarised in Chapter 7 on the 15 years follow-up data, it may be possible to claim that environmental design is of fundamental importance in both creating opportunities for crime and its control.

Secondly, in the past we have tended to see criminal behaviour as a series of different types of criminal event that tend to occur in all situations. But the evidence presented here seems to suggest that different types of crime, such as different types of burglary, should be seen as a response to different kinds of vulnerability presented by the environment. Burglary involving heavier spoils tends to take place in the most vulnerable locations, whereas in less vulnerable settings the burglars only take small valuable objects such as cash and jewellery. The process seems to be the opposite of the idea behind displacement theory in which prevention measures are designed to block or drive away a potential criminal attack. In this model the environment plays the opposite role; if it is vulnerable it attracts a criminal attack, but if it is well-designed criminal attacks do not arise. In essence, badly designed layouts attract crime, but if they are well designed the criminal is never tempted. No doubt the mechanism is continually reinforced, so an area will gain a reputation or image of a safe neighbourhood, rarely attracting crime as it presents few easy targets and little reward. A badly designed environment will gradually suffer more and more crime.

However, these are comments in passing. It is not really the purpose of this report to draw out more general theoretical propositions, but it does suggest that there is scope for further steps in developing more radical environmental theories of crime control.

Barry Poyner

Acknowledgements

The author would like to express his appreciation for all those who have given help and support in initiating and facilitating this research project.

Barry Webb, Deputy Director, Jill Dando Institute, University College London.
Paul Ekblom and Mark Bangs from the Home Office.

Sharon Henley – Architectural Liaison Officer, Northamptonshire Police.
John Mills – Architectural Liaison Officer, Essex Constabulary.
David Keenan – Research Officer, Chelmsford Police, Essex Constabulary.
Dr Tim Pascoe – Fire and Risk Sciences Division, BRE.
Lindsey Richards – Planning Officer, Northampton Borough Council.
Bob Torrell – Engineers Department, Northampton Borough Council.
Stephen Town – Architectural Liaison Officer, West Yorkshire Police.
Kay Trilk – Knowledge Manager, Northamptonshire Police (now with Northampton County Council).
John White – Architectural Liaison Officer, Hertfordshire Constabulary.
Kirsteen Wilkes – Research Officer, Hemel Hempstead. Hertfordshire Constabulary.

My wife, Ann, for her help and support not only with this book but throughout my career.

I thank my family for their love and support

This book is dedicated to my grandchildren
Megan, Adam, Katie and Harry

Crime Free Housing was published in 1991 (Poyner and Webb). It presented findings from a research study into the influence of housing design and layout on crime. The research was funded by the Home Office with further sponsorship from the house-building industry.[1] This report reviews these findings in the light of more recent research, comment and related developments in housing design policy, to set out an up-to-date view of the role of design and layout in creating safe residential areas virtually free of crime.

Since Oscar Newman wrote his famous book *Defensible Space* in the early 1970s, there had been considerable interest in the idea of using design to reduce crime in residential communities (Newman, 1973). Most of the attention of researchers was drawn to the problems of medium- and high-rise apartment buildings in the public housing sector, which was the initial focus of Newman's work. In Britain, the focus became the issue of vandalism on public housing estates; see for example Sheena Wilson's study of 'Vandalism and "defensible space" on London housing estates' (Wilson, 1980). Other ideas about crime prevention through environmental design (CPTED) became popular, particularly in the United States, for example by restricting access to residential neighbourhoods by road closures. For a review of these developments see *Design against Crime* (Poyner, 1983).

Less attention had been given to the design and layout of housing developments. This may be due to the general view that low-rise housing developments were generally less likely to have crime problems than medium- and high-rise public housing estates. Indicative of this view is the decision during the 1970s in Manchester to abandon the building of high-rise housing for the public sector and only build houses. However, by the early 1980s, when the research for *Crime Free Housing* was being planned, it seemed clear that future residential development would be dominated by low-rise housing and the private house-building industry.

Another issue made it even more urgent to look into the effect of design and layout on crime. Evidence was emerging from reputable criminological research that design and layout might be a more effective means of reducing crime than relying only on the conventional approach adopted by the security industry of strengthening doors, windows and locks (target-hardening). This security approach was most clearly reflected in the British Standard Guide for Security of Dwellings (BSI, 1986) and much similar advice and guidance was made available by the Home Office, police crime prevention services and the insurance companies.

When Maguire and Bennett interviewed house burglars about their crime methods, it became clear that the amount of target-hardening did not significantly affect their choice of target. One interviewee pointed out that 'burglars usually get in through back windows, which are out of sight of the street: therefore it can hardly be the sight of the insecure entry point which sparks off the idea to break in'. Their choice was based much more on particular kinds of area, where they may be familiar with the layout of streets and alleys or the general habits of people living there (Maguire and Bennett, 1982: 81–2).

Their doubts about the importance of target-hardening were reinforced in a contemporary study by Home Office researchers Winchester and Jackson (1982). In a survey comparing a sample of vic-

---

1. The original publication of *Crime Free Housing* was only made possible with financial support from Sir Clifford Chetwood (then Chairman and Chief Executive of George Wimpey PLC), from the Housing Research Foundation and from Mr and Mrs J. A. Pye's Charitable Settlement.

timised households with a general household sample, there was no evidence to suggest that better security (alarms, mortice deadlocks and window locks) reduced the risk of burglary. However Winchester and Jackson did find considerable differences in levels of victimisation between different house designs and settings. For example, detached houses were found to be more at risk that semi-detached houses, and houses in long terraces were less victimised than those in short terraces. They also identified 14 variables more associated with victimised houses than with non-victimised houses. Examples included 'not overlooked at the front by other houses', 'not overlooked on either side by other houses', 'access from front to back at both sides of the house' (ibid: 39).

Not only was it becoming clear that research needed to look at the design and layout of housing, it was also clear that research should consider all potential residential crime. To date only burglary had been considered in relation to houses. Indeed, it is only the crime of burglary that is specifically divided into residential and non-residential classifications in crime statistics for England and Wales. Vandalism and violence have been considered in high-rise estates, and it was known that car crime occurs in residential environments as well as elsewhere.

So, the original study that led to *Crime Free Housing* was unique in two important respects. It was:

1. The first study that specifically set out to investigate the relationship between housing layout and crime.

2. The first study to attempt to identify the full range of officially recorded crime that occurs in residential situations.

While the research was in progress and *Crime Free Housing* was being prepared for publication, there were signs that innovations in design guidance for crime prevention in housing developments were beginning to emerge. The National House-Building Council set up a working party to draft 'guidance on how the security of new homes can be improved' (NHBC, 1986). It was largely derived from the BSI Guide (BSI, 1986) but included references to on-curtilage parking and providing a securely gated access to a rear private yard or garden. Both of these recommendations arose from the research in hand. Brief guidance also appeared from the Department of Environment that focused more directly on design and acknowledged our own research, the NHBC and help from crime prevention officers in both Cheshire and Surrey Constabularies (Bennett et al, 1984).

However not all guidance was pushing in the same direction as our research. Warren and Stollard (1988) compiled an extensive review of literature and guidance on crime and housing but did little to resolve the many differing views that they encountered. They begin their summary of conclusions with the sentence –

> *The apparently opposing options which are advocated in order to achieve security through design have been discussed in this paper. Where disagreement exists ... no one design option has been chosen as the best solution, since there are no simple pattern book directives.*

Unintentionally they made a strong case for a more evidence-based set of research findings about crime and design.

A dramatic intervention came from Alice Coleman in 1987, when she published a short article in *House Builder* demanding 'More Sensitive House-Design Criteria *Please!*' (Coleman, 1987). In the article she listed 12 design features which largely imply that new housing should be similar to the typical 1930s semi-detached houses. She appears to claim that the use of these features in housing improvements have –

... produced effects as varied as the reduction or elimination of crime, the cessation of vandalism and racial harassment, the conversion of menacing gangs of children into polite individuals, the alleviation of certain mental illnesses and substantially reduced costs of estate management.

The problem with this extraordinary set of claims for 1930s suburbia is that there is little published *crime* data to support them. The only evidence cited in *Utopia on Trial* to compare good and bad house designs is the existence or absence of litter in front gardens (Coleman, 1985: tables 10, 12 and 13). For example, the recommendation that front gardens should be at least three metres front to back is derived from the finding that houses with shorter gardens have more litter.

This makes the case for a more rational approach to research and the need to ensure that design and layout recommendations should be related to actual crime. It was for this reason that support for the publication of *Crime Free Housing* was willingly given by the house-building industry.

Continuing development of guidance

Although *Crime Free Housing* was published commercially by Butterworth-Architecture, a well established publisher of design guidance for architects and planners, it was not a good time to interest designers in the importance of design in reducing crime and back it up with serious evidence-based research. This was a time of recession in the construction industry, when it would always be more difficult to sell books to architects and planners, particularly on a subject such as crime reduction.

Although the design and planning professions may have shown little enthusiasm for designing out crime in the early 1990s this was not the case for the police. In 1989 a police initiative called Secured by Design (SBD) was launched jointly by ten police forces in the South East. It was set up as a system for offering police approval for new developments. Although intended to cover any design project it was initially aimed at housing with its own design guidance. This was based on the BSI Guide, the NHBC recommendations and other existing police guidance. Although much of the guidance related to conventional target hardening for doors and windows and alarm systems, already well established in police crime prevention advice, the advice also included recommendations on housing layout. The illustration given was of a small cul-de-sac layout with a number of detached and semi-detached houses grouped around it.[2]

Although research findings from *Crime Free Housing* would predict that such a layout was unlikely to suffer from serious crime problems, it may be that this image of cul-de-sac design would later lead to a wider attack from the new urban design movement on cul-de-sac planning and police advice. The SBD initiative was established nationally under the aegis of the Association of Chief Police Officers. The guidelines continued to be developed and revised through the 1990s. Current versions of the SBD guidance are now available online at the following website: www.securedbydesign.com. Although available for all housing developers, in practice it is generally limited to social housing as it is a requirement adopted by the Housing Corporation.

In 1994 the Department of the Environment published a Circular (5/94) *Planning Out Crime*. This was the first major step towards involving the planning system in crime reduction policy. It

2. Tim Pascoe's study of the police view on guidance for Secured by Design reveals that there were differences of view about a more flexible set of guidance and the implicit recommendation for cul-de-sac layouts (Pascoe, 1993).

made it clear that when considering planning applications local authority planners should consider the potential implications for crime and crime prevention. The document itself does not make any dramatically new proposals for guidance, but it does briefly summarise some current ideas for use in planning out crime and provides a fairly comprehensive list of references to the key publications available at that time. However, the most important contribution of this Circular was that it began the slow process of involving planning professionals in crime reduction.

Although Circular 5/94 was an important step in developing the relationship between the police and planners, it was not until the introduction of the Crime and Disorder Act 1998 that this relationship became more active and influential. Certainly, in some parts of the country there is active involvement of police officers (architectural liaison officers and community safety officers) in new planning activities and a willingness on behalf of local authority planning staff to consult the police whenever issues of crime or disorder arise.

Through the 1990s there was a growing interest in rethinking the current approach to planning, to turn away from a wasteful suburbia to a more mixed use urban style of development. Perhaps this was typified by the work of the Urban Villages Group (Aldous, 1992). This growing demand for better quality development, and the need to solve problems of finding space for the ever increasing need for housing, has led to a new government design agenda. The key document is PPG3 (DETR, 2000a) and this is accompanied by a number of other guidance reports, in particular *Better places to live* (DTLR/CABE, 2001). In essence, the new government design agenda for housing seeks better design quality, better use of land, an emphasis on using brownfield sites, and reduction in car use by encouraging the use of public transport and creating walkable neighbourhoods.

This new urban design agenda will, no doubt, have implications for crime. There may be some advantages from the likely return of traditional street designs but the problem of providing for the car may still remain in many places. However, what is also happening is that more and more designers are being involved in the design of housing. The *RIBA Journal* reported a huge increase in the value of new private house commissions for architects following the publication of PPG3 even though the private housebuilders were building fewer homes than the previous year (Birkbeck, 2001). The desire to employ more professional designers suggests that developers are increasingly aware of the need for better design quality. It also suggests that the number of designers who will need to consider the implications for designing out crime in housing is increasing.

Developments in research

Alongside the development in guidance has been a rather modest flow of research relating to crime and environmental design. Some papers have been published that seem to support the findings in *Crime Free Housing*. For example, Beavon et al (1994) show that less accessible residential streets have less crime than through thoroughfares. But this seems to contradict the findings of Hillier and Shu (2000) who launched an attack on the idea of cul-de-sac designs. This issue needs to be given proper consideration, particularly as it ties in closely with the issue of permeability which seems to be a central precept of the new urbanism.

Yet another issue of lighting residential streets has been heavily researched and publicised by Kate Painter with the backing of the lighting industry (Painter, 1999). Such a topic was not dealt with in the original housing layout studies but justifies some response in this update. A short note on fear and lighting is given at the end of Chapter 7.

There are other sources of research evidence that have some influence on the revised thinking contained in this report. Some are new, such as the more recent papers that continue to discuss the Newman theory of territoriality that was so important to his 'defensible space' theory. There is also other older research that can be revisited in the light of later rethinking. This is discussed wherever appropriate throughout the report.

Finally, the very fact that this update of *Crime Free Housing* has been undertaken has led to a full reworking of the original analysis. One or two new questions have been asked of the old data set, but perhaps more exciting for the author has been the opportunity, supported by Northampton planners and engineers and police, to be able to examine changes made to some of the housing, and to obtain recent crime data, 15 years on from the original fieldwork. All this has meant that the current presentation of findings in this report, while broadly the same as the original, have been quite significantly updated and made more relevant to today's circumstances.

Form of the report

The form of the report broadly follows the structure of *Crime Free Housing*. It first discusses residential crime statistics. Then each type of crime is discussed in turn within three chapters:

Burglary and housing layout;

Car crime and housing layout; and

Theft and damage around the home.

Two chapters follow to present the study data 15 years on and three case studies. The final chapter attempts to summarise the findings on design and layout in terms that designers can use to develop appropriate prevention strategies for each project.

A crucial aim of the research that led to *Crime Free Housing* was to understand more clearly what constitutes residential crime. Until very recently official statistics for England and Wales only differentiated residential and non-residential crime in relation to burglary, and so for many, residential crime was assumed to be burglary ('burglary in a dwelling'). Recently, a second important category of 'criminal damage to a dwelling' has been separately identified in the statistics since 1998/9. There are other crimes associated with residential development such as car crime and thefts in and around housing. The British Crime Survey suggests that, in the year 2000, two-thirds of all vehicle theft occurred at the victim's home or in the street nearby (Kershaw et al, 2000: table A5.6). However, in other categories of crime it is impossible to tell from published statistics what proportions of crime are associated with housing design and layout. No doubt these more recent developments in identifying residential crime are in part attributable to the data published in *Crime Free Housing*.

To gain a clearer picture of residential crime, the starting point for the original research was to examine the crime record to see what could be identified as residential crime. Two very different areas were chosen. One was a large section of the London Borough of Harrow including five wards – Kenton East and West, Centenary, Wemborough and Stanmore Park, and the other was the town of Northampton.

The first four wards in Harrow represented typical semi-detached private sector housing built between the First and Second World Wars, in areas served by new extensions of the London Underground. It was also decided to include Stanmore Park as this was a distinctively up-market housing area. Maguire and Bennett (1982) had identified the higher risk associated with such areas, where the more 'professional' burglars are likely to be attracted with the prospect of more luxurious high value goods such as furs, silverware and antique clocks. All files for crime recorded in 1982 for the five wards in Harrow were examined and yielded a sample of 1508 recorded crimes.

The town of Northampton was selected for very different reasons. It was a relatively self-contained urban area well away from London which had been designated a 'new town' and undergone a huge amount of new development. It appeared to offer the opportunity to look at crime patterns for the whole town as well as an opportunity to look at the effect of recently built housing in both the public and private sectors. Since the size of the town would generate too much crime for us to handle (note that at that time most crime data was still processed manually and had not been computerised), a sample of 1 in 10 crimes was extracted from police files which amounted to a total of 1299 crimes.

The two samples where then re-classified manually, to work out a more helpful split between residential and non-residential crime. The resulting classification is set out in Appendix 1 at the end of the report. Observant readers will be quick to see that the equivalent table in *Crime Free Housing* was simplified and only the Northampton data was used. The reason for this was that the book focused mainly on the eastern district of Northampton rather than Harrow, but on reflection it seemed worth publishing here data from both areas based on the early unpublished research report (Poyner, Helson and Webb, 1985). Even now, 17 years on, it is rare to see such a detailed breakdown of the crime record. It may be of interest to many readers to see the range of crimes represented.

So what does the classification in Appendix 1 tell us about residential crime as a proportion of crime as a whole. Table 2.1 (below) summarises the principal categories. In a predominantly residential area such as Harrow more than half of all recorded crime is residential. For Northampton, about a third is residential. This is perhaps more typical of national crime figures as it represents a fairly balanced combination of town centre development with local centres and residential areas. Also included are recreational, entertainment and industrial developments.

Table 2.1   Comparison of residential and non-residential crimes in 1982 crime data

Crime category (All figures are expressed as a percentage)	Harrow res.	Harrow non-res.	N'pton res.	N'pton non-res.
Burglary	27.3	10.0	12.2	10.4
Theft (excluding vehicle crime)	5.3	8.8	7.8	18.9
Violent crime	0.4	4.6	0.5	4.8
Malicious damage	5.9	4.4	1.4	4.0
Theft of vehicles	8.1	3.3	6.2	6.2
Theft from vehicles	7.4	4.2	5.4	5.4
Malicious damage to vehicles	3.6	0.7	1.3	1.3
Other	–	3.7	–	8.8
Not classified	–	2.5	–	5.3
Totals (rounding errors not corrected)	58.0	42.2	34.8	65.1

Table 2.1 confirms the importance of burglary in a residential area such as a London suburb and to a slightly lesser extent to Northampton residential areas. The issue of car theft is also important in both areas alongside other theft in and around housing. Malicious damage is clearly a problem more for Harrow. Perhaps it is worth noting that much of this damage appears to be the result of interpersonal disputes. In the case of the Harrow data there was good evidence that many of these involved racial victimisation, particularly in an area such as Kenton East, where at that time the Asian population made up more than a quarter of local residents. At that time it was not police practice to formally record racial victimisation of this kind. Again this is a more recent change in official statistics (see Simmonds et al, 2002).

Violence is not seen as a major issue in residential crime. The figures shown in Table 2.1 for violence in a residential setting are for domestic disputes which while certainly taking place in the home are probably not likely to be resolved by design improvements. More noteworthy was the finding that no non-domestic violent assaults or sexual assaults occurred in residential settings. These were confined to other environments.

Crime Free Housing also presented the statistics for residential crime in terms of the number of crimes per 1000 dwellings. The data presented came not only from the 1982 study but also from a detailed study of crime in north-east Northampton in 1987, which was carried out in preparation for *Crime Free Housing*. This table is located in Appendix 2. Most of the categories have similar levels of crime in both Harrow and Northampton, but a few have clear differences. Some of these differences will be considered where appropriate later in the report but the following seem to deserve noting here. During the 1980s Northampton still had a major problem with gas and electric meters being broken open. There were very few of these crimes in Harrow, due no doubt to the fact that this form of pre-payment was no longer in use. It seems quite likely that the problem has greatly reduced in Northampton by now with continual modernisation of these utilities payment systems. There was more theft from around the home in Northampton. Research indicated that the layout of housing in some estates gave much more access to rear garden spaces in Northampton than the semi-detached style of housing with much more protected rear gardens. The other main difference related to car crime which was almost twice the level in Northampton than in Harrow.

Before moving on, it seemed worth asking if these patterns of residential crime are likely to have changed since 1982 and 1987. Even though there are no national statistics on residential crime other than burglary in a dwelling, it may be worth checking the overall pattern of change in the recorded crime figures. Table 2.2 shows the principal categories of crime used in national crime statistics and the levels of recorded crime in England & Wales for 1982, 1987 and 2001/2 (more recent data is published for the financial year instead of the calendar year).

It is clear from the figures in Table 2.2 that general proportions in crime categories have changed in the last 17 years. In 1982 residential burglary made up 12.5% of the crime record whereas more recent figures show it down to 9%. A similar change has occurred to theft of vehicles from over 10% down to 6.7%. However, although we know that recorded crime levels generally increased to a peak in the early 1990s and then began to drop, the total number of thefts from cars is now at a similar level to 1987 and other theft, criminal damage and violence have greatly increased. Although recent changes in the counting rules explain some of these increases it seems likely that the main reason for these increases is increased reporting and recording of these categories.

The general conclusion from these statistics seems to be that residential burglary and both forms of car theft remain major categories of crime and still deserve continued effort to reduce them. Some increase in criminal damage and theft may have occurred in residential crime but this might be due to changing recording practices. The biggest change in the pattern of crime seems to be in greatly increased recording of violence, but this is a category with very limited implications for residential crime. It seems reasonable to conclude that the priorities for crime reduction in the design and layout of housing remain little changed since the original studies in the mid-1980s.

Table 2.2 Trends in recorded crime in England & Wales 1982–2002

Crime category	1982 number	%	1987 number	%	2001/02 number	%
Residential burglary	407,000	12.5	483,000	12.4	426,872	9.0
Non-residential burglary	389,300	12.2	417,100	10.7	447,562	9.4
Theft (excluding vehicle crime)	995,700	29.3	1,003,800	25.8	1,214,774	25.6
Violent crime	151,200	4.6	198,800	5.1	650,154[1]	13.7
Criminal damage	417,800	12.8	589,000	15.1	1,064,470	22.4
Theft of vehicles	351,200	10.8	389,600	10.0	316,404	6.7
Theft from vehicles	449,000	13.8	658,600	16.9	655,127	13.8
Total recorded crimes	3,262,400		3,892,200		4,742,363	

[1]A major change in statistics has been the inclusion of common assault as violent crime

Comparing housing layouts

3

The classification of crime, described in the previous chapter, represents the results of the first stage of the research study using 1982 crime data. There are two very important reasons why this reclassification of crimes is so useful. The first is that it gives a clearer picture of what is residential crime and what crime is most likely to be influenced by housing layout and design. The full implications of what is presented in the classification about residential crime have still to be recognised by planners, urban designers, architects and developers. Too many still believe that preventing residential crime is primarily a matter of security against burglary.

The second and less obvious value of a good classification of crime is that it helps identify distinct issues for preventive treatment or intervention. The classification in Appendix 2 proposes a number of relatively sizeable groups of crimes, that might be used in the following analysis, but which have not previously been applied to studies of housing layout and crime. For example, the category of residential burglary has been further divided into luxury goods, electrical goods and cash and jewellery. As will be seen, by doing this some further insight can be gained into the conditions required for these crimes to occur. Few environmental design studies look at car crime and none present the thefts *from* and thefts *of* cars as separate types of crime, even though this is well established for research on car crime in general. The whole issue of theft from sheds, garages and gardens had never been considered until the 1985 report was presented (Poyner, Helson and Webb, 1985). Even now (2002) no other research on housing and crime has attempted to add to or revise these crime categories.

Visiting the scenes of crime

Essential to research using this classification approach is the need to visit the locations where the crimes occur. Many research techniques, such as interview surveys of victim experiences and computer-generated crime mapping, neglect the rich source of data that is the situation in which crime occurs. Information about the physical circumstances of a crime are rarely recorded in police files and so the influence of physical factors tends to be overlooked and only retained in the minds of local officers familiar with the ground. It is important to state that throughout the research described below a considerable amount of fieldwork was undertaken. By the end of each stage the research team had a very detailed knowledge of the research locations.

The early research on Harrow

One of the main reasons for selecting the Harrow area for the first stage of the research was to look at an established and fairly uniform area of housing to examine the extent to which detailed features of the layout might be influencing crime. For example, various claims had been made for cul-de-sacs being safer than through-roads, houses on corners might be more vulnerable and shared driveways may contribute to burglary risk by allowing open access to back gardens.

Some of these vulnerable physical characteristics could be readily associated with crime. For example, in a sample of 32 houses in Harrow from which higher value burglaries of luxury goods had been taken, 26 were large detached houses with ample space at the side to allow access to the back. Eight of the houses were corner houses with the side of the plot exposed to the side road. Seven had gardens backing onto open ground (wooded areas or a golf course).

Taking another sample of 70 semi-detached houses that suffered from burglaries of electrical goods in Harrow, 44 were found to have been entered from the rear or side of the house. Of these 18 had shared driveways often with little security to prevent access to back gardens, 5 had a clear through access to the rear and 10 had one side of their garden exposed (e.g. corner plots). Five houses looked secure and six were never visited. All these preliminary analyses indicated very similar results to those of Winchester and Jackson (1982).

Although these were encouraging findings, the research team discovered a major snag in the argument. The more they looked at all the housing in the same area as the victimised houses the more they realised that a great proportion of the housing was also vulnerable. So a check was made to see if burgled houses were more vulnerable than other neighbouring houses. Samples of houses were randomly selected from 100-metre squares on ordnance survey maps (scale 1:1250). Out of 1199 semi-detached houses 577 (48%) had shared drives. This was almost exactly the same proportion of shared drives as in the sample of burgled houses above (47%). In other words the proportion of shared drives in a random sample was the same as in the burgled sample.

The same idea was checked out for other likely variables, including the presence of side alleys and paths along the back garden fences and comparisons of houses in cul-de-sacs with houses in through-streets. In short, we came to the conclusion that trying to compare the vulnerability of individual houses and the risk of burglary was not going to be fruitful. Gradually we came to realise that instead of considering the vulnerability of individual houses, we should consider the vulnerability of each area or neighbourhood. The reason why Harrow was not revealing victimised houses as especially vulnerable was because the area was relatively uniform in design and layout. It looked as if the risk was much the same for all houses in an area and that they were targeted on a relatively random basis.

It was the Northampton crime data that most suggested the idea that what mattered more was the vulnerability of an area of housing rather than the vulnerability of each house. It was when the researchers looked at car crime that this became very clear. In visiting locations of car theft they repeatedly found themselves going to similar types of location. Most of the thefts had taken place in communal parking lots at the side or rear of terraced housing. There were several areas of housing with this kind of design, while others had completely different arrangements of parking – some on the street, some with parking on private driveways etc.

We soon realised that the layout planning of new housing in the north-east of Northampton was made up of many smaller patches of development each with different layout forms. If we adopted this part of Northampton as a research resource, it would be possible to treat these separate patches of development as a series of demonstrations in alternative ways of layout planning and design. Each of these could be analysed for levels of risk for different types of crime.

The Northampton methodology

The 1982 sample of crime data for Northampton was designed to gain an understanding of the patterns of residential crime for the whole town. Unfortunately that had meant that only a 10% sample was available. It was clear that, to make a more convincing analysis of crime for each of the development patches in north-eastern Northampton, a sample of at least one full year of crime was required. It was this need for more data that led to the extended timescale for the whole project. Although the first research report (Poyner, Helson and Webb, 1985) presented some indication of how this analysis might develop, it was decided that more funding should be sought to obtain a full year's sample for the north-eastern study area and to develop the findings into a book (*Crime Free Housing*).

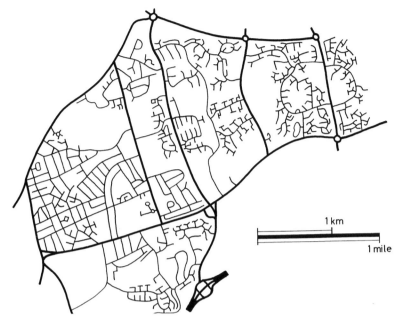

Figure 3.1   Area of eastern Northampton chosen for detailed study.

Unlike the part of Harrow chosen for the first study, the north-eastern side of Northampton represents a continuing development of the town over most of the 20th century. At the western end nearest the town centre is a grid pattern of streets built mainly before 1914, then further grid streets built in the 1920 and 1930s. Further developments during the 1960s and early 1970s fill in the space between the earlier developments and the main north–south route that divides the map into the east and west halves. The area to the east has the most spidery road pattern of loop roads and cul-de-sacs. Most of this was constructed from 1975 to 1990 under the New Town Corporation's initiative.

The map was then divided up into areas of like development. The task is more easily understood by visiting the area than by diagramming or written explanations. Essentially, each of the areas can be recognised as tracts of uniform development. Often they are the result of an area constructed by one developer or a separate area of public sector housing. Generally, because each pattern of development would be designed by different architects or layout planners each patch looks quite distinct. The only way to map these areas and decide how the patches can be defined is by driving along virtually every street on the map. The boundaries to the areas may be back fences between developments or principal or loop roads or boundaries with open space or other non-residential development such as retail development or schools.

The pattern of these development patches is shown in Figure 3.2 below. The largest have about 1000 dwellings and the smallest have under 100 dwellings. It was decided to leave out of any statistical calculations patches with less than 100 dwellings, but they are retained on any crime maps that are included.

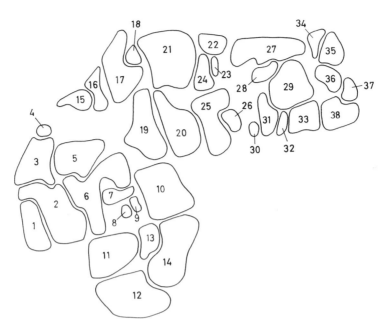

Figure 3.2   The north-eastern part of Northampton showing the Layout Areas to be used in the analysis.

Having defined these Layout Areas for the analysis the research team needed to record the typical characteristics of each patch. Since they were mainly interested in the idea of characteristics of the Layouts as a whole rather than of individual houses, it was somewhat easier to establish the key design characteristics of an area than to record individual details of each property. The latter would have required a huge amount of work, and no doubt this is why studies of this kind are rarely (or never) attempted.

In this series of studies, including the work conducted for this update, it has always been possible to check back for more details of each Layout Area whenever it is needed. A considerable advantage was gained when help in obtaining up-to-date maps was offered by the Borough Council. These maps show every house and its boundary, along with all details of roads and footpaths. This contrasted with a lack of up-to-date maps available in the early 1980s. Some of the most recent areas had only been completed a year or so before the study and at the time of the analysis work it was impossible to obtain maps for these areas.

Crimes were plotted on these maps in roughly the correct location. However, unlike the 1982 data it was no longer possible for the team to obtain full details of each crime due to the arrival of the Data Protection Act in 1984 (an inauspicious year to choose!). This Act, now replaced by the Data Protection Act 1998, prevented the police providing information (then computer based) that could identify individuals involved in crimes, which included victims. Although this legislative change had seriously restricted the scope of all crime research wishing to examine the crime environment, it was fortuitous that the method that had been devised for this second stage only required a general description of the location (i.e. in which Layout Area it had taken place). The issue being studied was the crime risk in contrasting types of housing layout. The team could function without details of the actual address. Comparisons between the crime risks for different Layout Areas were simply computed on the basis of crimes per 1000 households.

In the published data of *Crime Free Housing* there was some limited social data on the Layout Area, in that they were identified as being rented public sector or largely owner-occupied private sector housing. This update has tended to increasingly ignore the idea that tenure is a crucial issue in housing, due to the progressive selling of council housing. Although no comprehensive search for up-to-date information has been sought, there is an indication from a public sector estate just outside the study area of how far these sales have moved. Even though it had been one of the worst problem estates, over 60% of the houses are now owner-occupied.

Approach to analysis

Although what follows is not in quite the same format as the full data presentations of later chapters, it illustrates how the data is set up for comparisons between different aspects of design and layout. Table 3.1 takes three examples of Layout Areas from the map in Figure 3.2 and works out the rates for some of the larger crime sets in the classification presented in Appendix 2. The crime rates in term of crimes/1000 households/year are set out in tabular form for each crime type.

Table 3.1   Comparison of crime rates in three examples of different styles of layout (crime rates shown as crimes/1000 households)

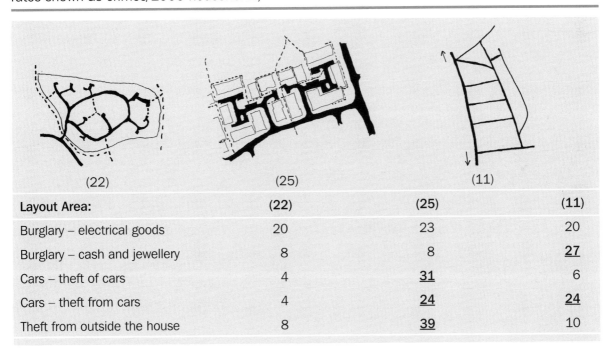

Layout Area:	(22)	(25)	(11)
Burglary – electrical goods	20	23	20
Burglary – cash and jewellery	8	8	**27**
Cars – theft of cars	4	**31**	6
Cars – theft from cars	4	**24**	**24**
Theft from outside the house	8	**39**	10

The differences in the crime rates between different Layout Areas are surprising. Where there are high and low rates, the high crime rates are emphasised in bold and underlined. There must be a reason why some areas have high rates and others low rates. The more traditional sociological approach to variations between crime levels in different neighbourhoods would look for differences in social and economic conditions to explain crime. A high crime area might be supposed to be socially deprived or even wealthier than surrounding areas because it presents more targets for theft. However, this kind of explanation does not seem to be very helpful at explaining these differences in more detail.

For example, Layout Area 22 appears to have generally less crime but shares similar levels of burglary with Area 25. Area 11 has much the same burglary of electrical goods but a much higher level of burglary of cash and jewellery. The pattern of car crime is also unexpected. Areas 25 and 11 have the same high levels of theft *from* cars but quite different levels of theft *of* cars. This last point cannot be explained logically by any socio-economic factors but it can be explained through the design and layout of the housing.

Thefts *from* cars are easier to commit than thefts *of* cars. The offenders may just snatch an external component or break a window and reach into a car. This can be done easily in Area 25 where cars are parked in internal parking courts surrounded by high fences and many alleyways leading to easy escape routes. In Area 11 many cars are parked on the street or private driveways surrounded by mature trees and shrub planting to provide plenty of cover. The street network gives plenty of through pedestrian movement on a natural line of movement in/out of town along a main road from the town centre. It may well be that planning a road network alongside a main route, such as in Area 11, makes it relatively easy for potential offenders to turn off the main through route into a side street where targets may be plentiful.

Area 22 has a low level of these thefts because most cars are parked on private driveways with relatively open and easily supervised front gardens. Furthermore, even though this cul-de-sac system has a few paths leading through the housing area, they do not encourage much use as they do not lead to major movement routes and are not natural shortcuts.

The reason for Area 25 to be a target for thefts *of* cars must be that the unsupervised internal parking courts are places in which local youths can attempt to start a car without looking especially suspicious, surrounded by many other cars which are often older and in less good working order. Police cars are unlikely to drive into these courts at night and if the potential offenders are disturbed their escape through the network of alleyways is easily achieved. Neither of the other two Areas 22 and 11 provide such ideal conditions for crime.

Finally, the reasons for Area 25 to be so vulnerable to theft from outside the house must be due to the lack of security that is given to front and back gardens. Front gardens are little more than small patches of plain grass opening directly onto a footpath along the front of each terrace. The back garden is always accessible from a footpath and often from the parking courts. The most convenient route from car to house is through the small back garden and it is easy to see when visiting that many of the gates in high fences are left open or insecure. By contrast the other two Areas 22 and 11 have larger rear gardens with no rear access.

The task of this research is to identify the layout and design patterns and features that seem to be most strongly related to the various crimes, in much the same way as described above. Figure 3.2 yielded 38 Layout Areas, but this included some which were too small to compute useful crime rates and so it was decided to leave out of the analysis any housing area with less than 100 dwellings. This produced a final sample of 31 areas. Inevitably the final selection of Layout Areas is somewhat limited because they are taken from an existing area of Northampton, but they do reasonably represent the range of layout types for housing used in England during the 20th century. Nevertheless, there will always be scope for further studies as new forms of residential planning emerge.

Burglary and housing layout

4

The relative importance of residential crime and residential burglary were discussed in Chapter 2 and the detailed numbers are set out in Appendices 1 and 2. The 1987 data applied specifically to north-east Northampton on which this study was focused. This fuller sample of data provided 608 crimes that could be classified as burglary under the classification. The analysis is shown in Table 4.1 below.

Table 4.1   Residential burglary for north-east Northampton for 1987

Crime type	Number of crimes	Rate per 1000 households	1982 rate
House burglary			
Luxury goods	8	0.6	0.0
Electrical goods	238	17.0	4.0
Cash and jewellery	103	7.4	4.7
Aggravated burglary	2	0.1	0.0
Burglary involving major damage	1	0.1	0.2
Unsuccessful attempts	148	10.6	5.3
Trivial and other	18	1.3	1.4
Insufficient information to classify	32	2.2	n/a
	550	39.3	15.6
Flats and residential institutions	14	1.0	0.9
Coin meter thefts	44	3.2	8.1
Total residential burglary	608	43.5	24.6

It is clear that the two main categories of 'electrical goods' and 'cash and jewellery' burglary cover the principal burglary problem. Although it is true that the large category of unsuccessful attempts is of interest to researchers, particularly those concerned with the effectiveness of security hardware, it was left out of the original analysis because it was impossible to know to which category it might have belonged if successful.

Other points include the fact that in a provincial town such as Northampton the issue of burglary of luxury goods, such as valuable carpets, pictures, silverware, clocks and antiques, is of relatively little important to crime statistics as a whole. The other category of thefts from coin meters, while included in burglary statistics, is a crime type best dealt with by the gradual elimination of meters (Hill, 1986). This was a problem in the 1980s that may be largely eliminated by now. It can be seen that it was more serious in the 1982 data than in the 1987 data. This could be due to the progressive elimination of meters.

Cash and jewellery burglary

While not as big a problem as electrical goods in the 1987 Northampton crime data, cash and jewellery burglary was a more important category in both Harrow and Northampton in the 1982 data. So, it is probably the more common form of domestic burglary and perhaps the most easily understood. It most likely involves a burglar wandering the streets looking for an opportunity to find a relatively easy way into an unoccupied house. His (nearly always a male) search for a suitable target is most likely made by walking familiar streets with plenty of houses, ideally in a well-heeled neighbourhood. Houses with front doors and access to the back around the side clearly present an opportunity, particularly if they have some trees or shrubs that screen the door from the street. Doors are knocked to check if the house is unoccupied and perhaps tried for resistance to pressure or else the burglar might try the side passageway, again a gate might be easy to open unobserved. The advantage of taking only cash and jewellery (including other small portable valuables) is that once back in the street, the burglar could carry off his spoils concealed in his clothing without appearing suspicious.

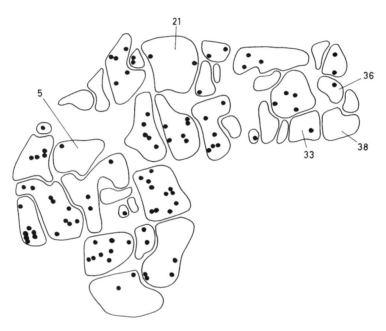

Figure 4.1   Distribution of cash and jewellery burglary for 1987

Figure 4.1 shows a relatively evenly distributed pattern of crimes. There are no very high concentrations, but there is a variation with several Layout Areas having no crime of this type and others having moderate levels. Taking only those Areas with over 100 houses, 9 out of 31 patches are free of cash and jewellery burglary.

The analysis of this distribution offered in *Crime Free Housing* suggested that the main characteristics of the Layout Areas that attracted this kind of burglary were:

Housing which is nearer the town centre

Housing areas with more road access points

Older houses

The presence of foliage at the front and long back gardens seems to assist the offender

Open side access to the rear is more important than back gates

Escape routes on foot are useful but not to reach a parked car

It went on to state that:

The relevance of these factors is easy to understand. Unlike electrical goods burglary, cash and jewellery is done on foot and housing nearer to the town centre may be more accessible to potential criminals. The street pattern is more accessible and strangers walking these streets will not arouse suspicion. If a target is selected and the intending burglar calls at the front door, foliage and an enclosed front garden will give some cover. If he finds no one at home, open access around the side of the house to a secluded back garden is ideal for this kind of crime. It is also possible that older houses are seen as easier to burgle because they may have less sound window frames and doors, and perhaps the older locking hardware is broken or well worn. Perhaps also older houses have more nooks and crannies and provide better picking for old jewellery and keepsakes, etc., compared with the life style of the new town houses with their videos and stereos. (Poyner and Webb, 1991: 59–60)

This was a clearly drawn picture of this kind of crime. The principal conclusions about prevention through design were to maximise the surveillance of the front door from neighbouring houses and to emphasise the importance of having a locked gate or doorway to create a secure side access to the back garden. One aim of this update is to re-examine the original analysis in the light of other research and planning developments in the hope of checking and, if possible, strengthening these findings.

Electrical goods burglary

This was the more common type of burglary in the Northampton data. It also seemed to be a more brazen pattern of criminal behaviour in that the thief or thieves would be carrying off larger and heavier objects. In most cases they will probably carry their spoils to a car or van parked discretely nearby.

The map in Figure 4.2 reveals a very different pattern of distribution to that in Figure 4.1. It is much more focused on the new housing built under the New Town Eastern District development from the mid-1970s. All this area had a network of footpaths providing traffic-free access to schools, local shopping and community facilities. The analysis presented in *Crime Free Housing* suggested that this kind of burglary occurred in housing areas distinguished by the following environmental characteristics:

New housing further from the town centre

Where there are pedestrian through routes

Where there is a lack of surveillance of roadways

Where houses do not face each other (front doors and windows)

Where there are back garden gates off footpaths

Where there are pedestrian escape routes to car parking

There is evidence to suggest that open-plan fronts are more vulnerable

Curiously the availability of side access from the front to the back was not very important in this data, which suggests that access was mainly from the rear in the Northampton study. Unlike cash and jewellery burglars, the electrical goods burglar would select a neighbourhood first, then find a suitable place to leave his car or van and then find a target on foot. From this point the approach might be similar to cash and jewellery but the escape to the car would make rear escape more desirable. Certainly in the Layout Areas from number 20 and over, there were many more opportunities to leave cars parked in relatively concealed locations, such as parking bays surrounded by overgrown shrubbery.

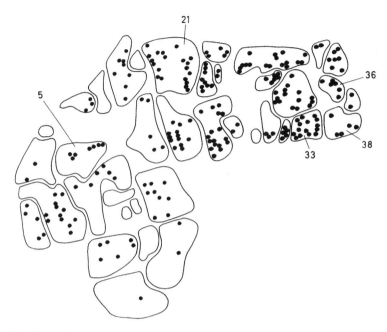

Figure 4.2   Distribution of electrical goods burglary in eastern Northampton for 1987

The view of this analysis in the original book was:

> ...*that surveillance should be maximised by making houses face each other across the street and overlook the access roads. Efforts should be made to avoid footpaths that create through pedestrian routes and provide foot-only escape routes to places where cars can be left ready for a get-away. It appears that a back gate should be avoided and a low wall around the front garden also helps to discourage this kind of burglary. Perhaps it helps to make an offender more obvious when leaving the premises carrying more bulky electrical goods. (Poyner and Webb, 1991: 58)*

Acceptability of these ideas at the time of publication

Taking the two types of burglary together, it seemed to imply that houses were best located in the traditional street form with a minimum of segregated footpaths and little opportunity to park in an anonymous or secluded place. At the time of writing the authors felt that such recommendations would have limited acceptance since the more progressive designers of the late 1980s had seemed bent on creating alternative forms of housing layout, whether grouped around greens or facing onto footpaths rather than streets with vehicle access. However, all this changed during the 1990s as the new urban design agenda has taken hold and the 'street' is now the new urban chic.

A similar trend has occurred in the provision of segregated footpath systems. The near obsession for separating traffic from pedestrian movement that dominated the New Town development of Northampton's Eastern District Plan has largely disappeared. Interestingly, the original book criticised two diagrams in the first edition of the Department of Environment's BD32 *Residential roads and footpaths* (Noble et al, 1977: 20) encouraging the idea of connecting ends of cul-de-sacs streets by footpaths to create useful walkable routes to facilities through a neighbourhood. In the second edition published soon after *Crime Free Housing*, these diagrams were removed, and the idea of segregated footpath networks seems to have been edited out. Nevertheless, government guidance on pedestrian routes and crime remained uncertain and resistant to the idea of trying to eliminate footpath systems. The more recent companion guide to BD32 *Places, Streets and Movement* states:

...If separate footpaths or cycle tracks form part of a layout they should be on routes which generate high levels of movement and should be as short as possible.

However, the statement continues:

Long, indirect pedestrian and cycle links may feel threatening for users, and may provide escape routes for criminals. (DETR 1998: 46).

New issues from research and the urban design agenda

Since the publication of *Crime Free Housing* in 1991 there has been relatively little research on the question of crime reduction through design and layout of residential areas. The principal exception is the work of Hillier and Shu (2000) which has raised the argument that cul-de-sac street layouts are undesirable and that through streets are safer. The issue is discussed further below. It also appears to conflict with research from British Columbia which suggested that property crime reaches higher levels on streets that are more accessible – i.e. they have more connections to other streets (Beavon et al, 1994).

This issue gains more significance when it is noted that the new urban design agenda aims to make urban residential areas more permeable to promote movement on foot and access to and from public transport. These ideas appear in design guides such as that produced for the redevelopment of Hulme in Manchester. 'All streets should terminate in other streets' and 'streets should encourage through movement' (Hulme Regeneration Limited, 1994: 22). Similar points are made in the government's recently published *Better places to live* (DTLR, 2001: 25), a companion guide to *Planning Policy Guidance Note 3: Housing* (DETR, 2000a). Here there is a clearly expressed preference for a grid-like layout over a cul-de-sac street system. Since *Crime Free Housing* was relatively neutral on the issue of cul-de-sacs, preferring to focus on the problem of footpaths linking cul-de-sacs, it seems to be an important issue with which to revisit the Northampton study.

Research on burglary continues to emerge from the criminological community, typically in the form of interviews with burglars. These provide supporting evidence on issues such as side access to the back garden (Evans and Fletcher, 1998) and the importance of screening foliage to give cover for burglars (Palmer et al, 2002). The more environmentally oriented researchers provide data from surveys of residents' experience (Rengert and Hakin, 1998 and Shaw and Gifford, 1994). The latter continue an interest in developing the defensible space theory in a series of studies of house vulnerability based on photographs and assessments made by burglars, residents and police officers (MacDonald and Gifford, 1989; Ham-Rowbottom, Gifford and Shaw, 1999). The problem for most of this research is that it is based on the opinions of those involved in crime (victims, offenders, etc.) rather than more directly on actual recorded incidents of crime that have taken place in specific environmental settings.

The British government's national Crime Survey, although not designed to deal with the issues in this report, has increasingly included questions that can have some bearing on the vulnerability of housing and on security provisions in typical households. These were helpfully summarised for burglary in a Home Office Statistics Bulletin on *Burglary of Domestic Dwellings* by Budd (1999). Other government initiatives also provide useful background experience on the prevention of burglary as in the Safer Cities Programme, reviewed by Ekblom and colleagues (1996). Another example of a crime prevention initiative that was well researched and draws attention to the problem of rear access to terraced housing is 'Alleygating' by the Metropolitan Police. Back alleyways of terraced streets were closed by installing locked gates, clearly reducing access to burglars (Beckford, circa 1995).

With all these developments in both research and published guidance, there is ample justification for revisiting the analysis of 1987 data in the Northampton study. No other study since then has included data from such a large area (about 14,000 households) with such diverse approaches to design and layout. The original analysis did not look at the issue of street pattern as much as more recent interest would demand. The diversity of recommendations that are evident from a review of the design guidance available to planners and architects also demands more evidence-based insight for those formulating new guidance.

Findings from a reworked analysis

Conventional security for houses

Before discussing the findings from the reworking of the data analysis in *Crime Free Housing* it is important to restate the underlying philosophy behind this work on layout and design factors in reducing crime. The idea is that if we can create a safe residential neighbourhood the need for conventional security measures on individual houses is greatly reduced. The normal response to concerns over increasing crime problems has been to instal security lighting, burglar alarms, window shutters and even closed circuit TV surveillance on public sector housing estates. Less technically sophisticated solutions include steel gates blocking rear access paths and barbed wire on top of rear garden walls and fences (examples of both can be found in the Northampton study area at the time of writing).

Objections to these heavier methods of security are of three principal kinds. The first is that they do not present a good psychological message for residents and visitors to an area and must contribute to the problem of fear of crime. Secondly, there are side effects that can create nuisance, for example the flashing on of bright security lights can be a direct nuisance to night-time traffic and it can irritate the innocent passer-by who simply wishes to take a dog for a walk after dark. Most obviously of all, there is the cost, not only of initial installation but of sustaining the measures. Alarm systems need routine maintenance and a back-up system. No doubt the main objection to electronic surveillance in residential areas is not just the cost of installation but also the continued expenditure on the running of a control centre.

Looking beyond Britain there are examples of housing developments where security measures are taken much further and yet illustrate the problem of cost and sustainability. Gated communities in the United States are now available to the middle class as well as the rich and famous.

They usually offer no amenities beyond a gated entry, perimeter fence, or perhaps a pool or tennis court. Home to young professionals and middle managers, they provide the cachet of exclusive living to those with nonexclusive incomes. Many have electronic gates, and others

have guardhouses at the main entrance. The gatehouse stands solely as a psychological deter-
rent to outsiders, as homeowners' associations sometimes never hire guards because of the
high ongoing cost. (Blakely and Snyder, 1998: 62)

There is a continuing trend to increase the amount of security to homes (Budd, 1999: table 5.5) but it is also true that the less well protected tend to be the poorer groups in the population. An interesting summary of the situation in some other countries appears in Mawby's book on *Burglary* (Mawby, 2001). Generally other developed countries have lower levels of security provision than Britain and there is evidence that in the developing world, the question of sustainability has more influence. He quotes from a UN source that 'the proportion of households in the developing world with alarms actually fell between 1992 and 1996, a trend ... attributed to maintenance problems and the lack of spare parts'.

It is difficult to be certain about the security measures required in a residential area designed under the recommended layout planning principles identified in this chapter. The chances are that current standards are on the generous side for the ideal setting because they have to be able to have some impact on the more insecure settings. Besides, anyone with experience of standards committees or working groups will be aware of the pressure from manufacturers to gain official recognition for higher specifications. It is a brave man in today's litigious world who guarantees a reduced standard of security equipment, but it seems reasonable to stick with the more common basics of robust door and window designs with good securing mechanisms that are easy to use. More elaborate security measures are probably unnecessary. Clearly simple design faults such as generous letter boxes that enable children to reach inside and unlock a front door have to be eliminated, but as the frequently used contemporary phrase goes, it's not rocket science!

The arguments rehearsed for increased measures are difficult to unravel since the research or survey data is derived from the real world in which layout and design issues are not controlled. However, there does seem to be something fairly fundamental about the need for basic security for dwellings. For example, in government-funded projects for improving burglary reduction in existing housing under the Safer Cities Programme, Ekblom and colleagues found that: 'Target-hardening reduced burglary under all conditions in which it was present.' (Ekblom et al, 1996: 42). In this context the measures were: 'outside doors strengthening or strengthening frames, with double locks or deadlocks, security chains or bolts, peep hole viewers; windows with security locks' (ibid: 68). It is also interesting to see from British Crime Survey findings that there were major differences in the amount of target-hardening between victim and non-victim households. Over 70% of non-victim households had deadlocks on doors and locks on windows whereas of victimised households only 41% had this protection. But when the same comparison is made for burglar alarms, there is much less difference between victimised and non-victimised households. Twenty-four per cent of non-victimised households had alarms, but 19% of victimised households also had alarms. This suggests that alarms, while becoming more common, have only a limited effect on preventing burglary (Budd, 1999: table 5.7).

Form of presentation of the analysis data

The method used to compare the various design and layout factors was a simple matrix showing which factors occurred in which Layout Areas. The analyses for the two forms of burglary are set out in separate matrices in Figures 4.3 and 4.4. Against the list of factors on the left, a series of columns for each Layout Area are arranged in rank order from the lowest to the highest crime rates. The crime rates for cash and jewellery burglary are generally much lower than for electrical goods burglary. As can be seen in Figure 4.4 there are 9 areas with a zero crime rate in cash and jewellery burglary with the crime rates for the other 22 areas ranging from 1 up to 27 crimes per 1000 houses. The pattern for electrical goods is only 3 no crime areas with the range of crime rates rising to 63 crimes per 1000 households.

Each matrix shows the average crime rate associated with each factor. Each factor will have its own distribution across the matrix. Where the factors are concentrated at the high or low ends of the horizontal rows in the matrix it will be relatively easy to come to some judgement about their relevance to prevention. Where a factor is distributed more equally across the horizontal rows in the matrix, it has to be assumed that it has a more neutral influence. One problem for interpretation is that if a factor is almost universally present in all housing areas it may be either irrelevant or essential to preventing crime.

The list of factors used in this reworked analysis was based on the original list in *Crime Free Housing* but with revisions determined by developments since its publication. The actual list presented here is the result of much trial and error in trying to define factors in such a way as to produce clearer and more discriminating distributions. The contents of the two matrices in Figures 4.3 and 4.4 are discussed one by one below.

Household income

The most common reason given to explain the distribution of crime in a residential area seems to be its social status. For example, an analysis by Budd (1999: 12) of burglary victims in the British Crime Survey quotes the categories of 'council estates and greatest hardship' and 'multi-ethnic, low income areas' as among the most victimised (13.2% and 10.1% respectively). The original analysis in *Crime Free Housing* attempted to explore the influence of social status by examining how the public-sector housing estates were distributed in terms of low and high burglary rates. Perhaps surprisingly, the findings in that analysis showed no evidence to support the idea that public-sector areas had higher burglary rates than owner-occupied areas. This was a useful finding in that it supported the idea that design and layout were more influential in determining crime rates than tenure.

In revisiting the study area 15 years later it seemed that the old dichotomy of public rented and private owner-occupied sectors has been undermined by the Thatcher government's policy of council house sales. The ubiquitous 'For Sale' boards on ex-public sector housing show that much of the previously rented public-sector housing is now owner-occupied. Indeed, as was noted earlier, one neighbouring ex-new-town estate is now more than 60% owner-occupied.

In view of these changes it seemed more appropriate to try a more direct set of categories that relate to wealth. A simple three-tier classification of upper-, middle- and lower-income households was used. This was a simple enough categorisation for judgements to be made for the purpose of the analysis. In the event, with the exception of area 31, all those classified as public-sector housing in the first study were classified as lower-income housing in this revised analysis.

From Figures 4.3 and 4.4, the levels of wealth do not, in general, influence the attractiveness of a Layout Area to burglary. There are middle- and lower-income Layout Areas across the spectrum of low to high crime rates. Indeed, the average crime rates for each category of income and crime level is around the average for each type of burglary. The one exception is that all but one of the five upper income areas have among the highest rates for cash and jewellery burglaries, with more than double the average crime rate (14.2 against the average for cash and jewellery of 6.2).

Figure 4.3 Analysis of design and layout factors for burglary – electrical goods

LAYOUT AREAS / CRIME RATES IN RANK ORDER	av. 16.9	7	13	16	12	3	6	14	5	15	31	34	2	1	19	10	21	17	26	11	22	20	27	29	35	25	38	36	32	28	33	24
		0	0	0	2	3	6	8	9	9	9	11	12	13	13	14	17	19	19	20	20	21	21	21	23	23	23	24	30	33	37	63
Household income																																
1. Upper-income households	14.0	X					X										X		X							X						
2. Middle-income households	17.8			X	X	X	X				X	X		X	X	X			X		X			X	X	X	X			X		X	X	X
3. Lower-income households	16.9	X						X	X				X				X					X		X	X	X	X			X		
Age and distance from town centre																																
4. Housing built before Second World War	10.9	X			X	X						X	X		X		X		X													
5. Outer suburban area – beyond the A43 main road	24.7								X			X				X		X		X	X		X	X	X	X	X	X	X	X	X	X
Through-streets and cul-de-sacs																																
6. Drive-through route	9.6	X	X	X	X	X	X		X	X		X	X			X							X		X							
7. Direct turning off a main road	10.7	X			X	X	X		X			X	X		X		X		X													
8. Grid streets (includes some short cul-de-sacs)	10.9	X			X	X						X	X		X		X		X													
9. Cul-de-sac road system (includes loop roads)	19.9		X	X					X	X		X			X		X		X		X	X		X	X	X	X	X	X	X	X	X	X
Footpath systems																																
10. Layouts with blind cul-de-sacs (no footpaths)	7.7	X	X	X								X		X			X															
11. Cul-de-sac roads linked to footpath networks	24.0								X		X		X		X		X		X		X	X		X	X	X	X	X	X	X	X	X	X	X
12. Pedestrian-only routes through the area	24.6					X				X		X		X		X		X				X		X	X	X	X	X	X	X	X	X	X
13. Pedestrian escape routes to unsupervised parking	26.4											X				X		X				X		X	X	X	X		X	X	X	X	X
Predominant house form																																
14. Terraced housing – mainly in rows of four or more	15.1	X				X			X	X	X	X	X	X			X		X			X		X	X	X	X			X		
15. Detached and semi-detached	18.8		X	X	X			X	X					X	X		X		X	X				X	X		X	X	X
Relation of houses to streets																																
16. Streets overlooked by houses along both sides	15.3	X	X	X	X	X	X	X	X	X	X	X	X	X	X	X		X	X	X				X	X		X	X	X	
17. Many houses facing across greens or footpaths	19.3							X	X						X					X		X	X	X	X		X	
18. Houses sometimes face the back of other houses	22.8														X				X			X	X		X	
19. Not all streets are overlooked by houses	26.6														X				X		X	X	X	X		X	
20. Higgledy-piggledy streets (odd angles and curves)	35.5						X							X				X						X	X		X	X	X	
Front gardens																																
21. Front foliage obscures front door and side access	10.1	X			X	X	X	X					X			X		X		X												
22. Front gardens boundary – fence/wall/hedge	9.7	X	X		X	X		X				X	X	X		X		X		X												
23. Front gardens 3–5 metres	16.0	X	X	X	X	X		X			X	X	X			X	X		X	X	X	X				X	X		X	X	X	
Access to back gardens/yards																																
24. Access at side of house – open/flimsy/recessed	16.3			X	X	X		X				X		X	X		X		X	X				X	X		X	X	
25. Pedestrian access to rear of garden (gate)	15.6			X			X	X	X			X			X	X		X		X	X	X	X		X	
26. Long/large back gardens	9.8	X		X	X	X						X	X		X	X										X	
27. All back gardens with full height fences	17.3	X	X	X	X	X	X	X	X	X	X	X		X	X	X	X	X	X	X	X	X	X	X	X	X	X	X	X	X	X	X
28. Gardens mostly back onto other gardens	9.3	X		X	X	X	X					X			X		X		X													
29. Density – over 30 per hectare	19.8	X		X			X	X	X			X		X	X		X				X			X	X	X	X		X	X	X	X	X

Figure 4.4 Analysis of design and layout factors for burglary – cash and jewellery

LAYOUT AREAS / CRIME RATES IN RANK ORDER	av. 6.2
Household income	
1. Upper-income households	14.2
2. Middle-income households	5.5
3. Lower-income households	4.3
Age, density and distance from town centre	
4. Housing built before Second World War	16.9
5. Inner suburban area – within the A43 main road	9.5
Through-streets and cul-de-sacs	
6. Drive-through route	6.4
7. Direct turning off a main road	12.4
8. Grid streets (some short cul-de-sacs)	13.1
9. Cul-de-sac road system (includes loop roads)	4.4
Footpath systems	
10. Layouts with blind cul-de-sacs (no footpaths)	9.2
11. Cul-de-sac road linked to footpath networks	4.2
12. Pedestrian-only routes through this area	4.6
13. Pedestrian escape routes to unsupervised parking	3.8
Predominant house form	
14. Terraced housing – mainly in rows of four or more	4.4
15. Detached and semi-detached	8.6
Relation of houses to streets	
16. Streets overlooked by houses along both sides	8.0
17. Many houses facing across greens or footpaths	4.2
18. Houses sometimes face the back of other houses	5.2
19. Not all streets are overlooked by houses	5.3
20. Higgledy-piggledy streets (odd angles and curves)	6.5
Front gardens	
21. Front foliage obscures front door and side access	10.7
22. Front garden boundaries – fence/wall/hedge	9.9
23. Front gardens 3–5 metres	6.2
Back gardens	
24. Access at side of house – open/flimsy/recessed	10.4
25. Pedestrian access to rear of garden (gate)	7.1
26. Long/large back gardens	10.8
27. Back gardens with full height fences (or walls)	6.6
28. Gardens mostly back onto other gardens	15.3
29. Density – over 30 per hectare	4.6

All that can be taken from this in terms of design recommendations is that:

Areas of high value housing will need to have the most careful treatment in terms of measures that are effective at preventing cash and jewellery burglary.

From a somewhat different perspective, it is worth noting that the distribution of lower income areas is widely spread (see Figure 4.5). If, as seems to be generally accepted by criminologists, offenders are more likely to live in lower income areas then most of the housing areas are close to such areas and in that sense vulnerable. Baldwin and Bottoms' classic study of crime in Sheffield reported that more than 50% of burglaries took place within a mile of the offender's home (Baldwin and Bottoms, 1976). Certainly in this Northampton study, all of the Layout Areas are within a mile of some lower income housing. Even so, there is just a possibility that areas 12 and 14 are slightly better protected as they are at the southerly limits of housing development in the borough.

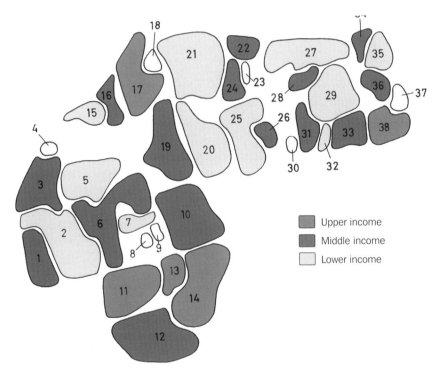

Figure 4.5 Distribution of upper-, middle- and lower-income levels in Layout Areas

Distance from town centre

Another common perspective on the distribution of burglary is that inner and older areas of towns and cities tend to have higher concentrations of crime. This would be explained in terms of environmental criminology and routine activity theory, which closely overlap in this context. For example, Paul and Patricia Brantingham in a paper called 'Notes on the Geometry of Crime' (1981/91) presented a set of diagrams showing how an offender's movement between home and work, shopping or entertainment might influence his search for criminal opportunities. Such a theory suggests that since much of these activities in a moderate sized town such as Northampton tend to focus on the centre, the concentration of crime would tend to increase nearer to the centre.

The analysis in *Crime Free Housing* examined distance from the town centre and the age of the property. Both generated clear crime patterns. The new housing developments further from the centre suffered much more electrical goods burglary (as is clear from the crime mapping in Figure 4.2 above), while cash and jewellery burglary occurred in older housing closer to the centre. The distance from the town centre is represented in a simplified form in Figures 4.3 and 4.4, by counting Layout Areas within the main A43 road as inner suburbs and beyond the A43 as outer suburbs. All the Layout Areas with high levels of electrical goods burglary are in the outer suburbs while most of the areas with higher levels of cash and jewellery burglary are in the inner suburbs.

On the face of it, this distribution suggests that the location of these crimes is not driven by a routine activity theory explanation – where offenders tend to move about during their normal life routines. More likely the pattern reveals that the kind of search strategy adopted by an intending burglar depends on the mode of access used – whether it is on foot or using a car or van. The inner suburbs have more grid-like streets easily accessed on foot and with some higher value property. The outer suburbs may involve longer distances for travelling but are easily explored by car, and a potential burglar can discreetly park in some secluded place with easy access to housing through a network of pathways.

Drive-through routes

Crime Free Housing did not analyse the relationship between crime and specific types of street pattern, although there was some attempt to compare the accessibility of each Layout Area in terms of the number of ways in by road and the extent to which the roads provided routes through the layout. The view taken at that time was that these were not major issues in the control of crime even though it could be claimed from the data that increased accessibility by road seemed to encourage burglary of cash and jewellery (Poyner and Webb, 1991: 57).

One of the principal reasons for ignoring the issue of 'through-roads' was that the study had been designed to look at the more detailed aspects of design and layout. In terms of the Northampton map, the main roads had been excluded from the Layout Areas. This is partly due to the fact that the newer main roads were constructed without direct access to housing. Older main roads were left out largely because of what had been previously reported in crime prevention research about through routes. This author had reviewed early research in the United States on the issue of 'Safer Neighbourhoods' which largely focused on the problem of crime being associated with too much through traffic (Poyner, 1983). It was claimed that the exposure to large numbers of outsiders in a drive-through neighbourhood promoted opportunities for crime.

Several examples of road closure as an anti-crime measure have been published in the United States. Oscar Newman offered his version of this in his second book *Community of Interest* (Newman, 1980), in which he reported on the private closure of residential streets in St Louis. Part of the purpose of that project was to avoid large traffic flows moving through residential streets. The Asylum Hill project at Hartford, Connecticut was another well-publicised early example of successful crime reduction in which diverting through traffic was a significant element (Poyner, 1983; Fowler and Mangione, 1982). More recent examples of road closure programmes are reported by Atlas and LeBlanc (1994) in the United States. These included a project called 'Operation Cul-de-Sac' by the Los Angeles Police and another at Miami Shores, both appearing to have an impact on burglary, larceny and auto-crime.

We might conclude therefore from research outside this study that:

There is a case for keeping major traffic routes away from residential areas and allowing only light through traffic.

In the analysis in Figures 4.3 and 4.4, line 6 looks at the role of through traffic routes in Layout Areas. Figure 4.3 shows that there is an advantage in having drive-through routes in Layout Areas if the aim is to reduce electrical goods burglary. Most of the areas with drive-through routes have low rates for electrical goods burglary and the average for line 6 is 9.6 against the average for all Layout Areas of 16.9. But there is no advantage for cash and jewellery as the average for this line in Figure 4.4 is 6.4 – virtually the same as the average rate for all areas (6.2 crimes/1000 households/year).

What does this mean? The reason why light through traffic discourages electrical goods burglary must be that there are more drivers and passengers moving through the area who might notice suspicious behaviour. Burglars carrying off various electrical goods are more likely to attract attention. Presumably the reason why cash and jewellery burglary is less affected by through traffic must be that the behaviour involved is less suspicious (not carrying any bulky items, only approaching the house from the front, no car parked nearby).

Clearly, in preventing burglary there is some advantage in light through traffic and no disadvantage providing heavily trafficked routes are excluded. So, it can be claimed that:

Residential areas will have less burglary if they include through traffic routes, providing they only carry local light traffic.

Line 7 of the two matrices presents the first example of directly conflicting findings. The idea of suggesting that easy access from main roads might increase the risk of burglary came from observing that some of the inner Layout Areas (notably Areas 1 and 11) were the worst examples of cash and jewellery burglary and they were directly accessible from turning immediately off main roads. The analysis in Figure 4.4 supports this observation with an average double the overall figure for the crime. On the other hand Figure 4.3 is the other way around. Electrical goods burglary is much lower in areas directly accessible from main roads (10.7 compared with the overall average of 16.7).

There are research results from elsewhere that support the importance of accessibility of main roads to crime. The pattern of cash and jewellery burglary appears to occur in an earlier study by Pascoe of burglary in Watford. He found that locations of many domestic burglaries were on or close to main thoroughfares, indicating that these offenders may prefer not to enter too far into a residential neighbourhood and retain the advantage of a quick escape (Pascoe, 1991: figure 3). An American study by Rengart and Hakin found that in Greenwich, Connecticut burglary was at a higher rate closer to highway exits (Rengert and Hakin, 1998).

However, since the evidence is not clearly working in the same direction for the two kinds of burglary we have to doubt that any recommendation can be made on this particular feature of accessibility.

Cul-de-sacs and through-streets

There has been speculation in Britain about the influence of cul-de-sac streets compared with through roads ever since the 1980s, long before the current advocacy of 'interconnected streets' as part of the designing out crime principles set out by Lord Rogers' Urban Task Force and quoted by Schneider and Kitchen (2002: 206) from *Towards an Urban Renaissance* (Urban Task Force, 1999). In 1989, a survey for the Housing Research Foundation reported the crime experiences of residents from several modern private-sector housing developments at Wokingham. The total area comprised about 1400 houses. The authors reported that dead-end streets had the lowest overall crime rate while through streets had the highest. The exception to this was for burglary. The result was clearly of interest but the total number of crimes involved was very small, making it impossible to draw strong conclusions (Noble and Jenks, 1989).

Also in 1989, the police launched their Secured by Design scheme in the South East of England, which became a national scheme in 1994. Early guidance produced for this scheme presented recommended good practice in housing design by illustrating a typical cul-de-sac development (see Figure 4.6). The emphasis on the cul-de-sac was confirmed in Topping and Pascoe (2000) who refer to the concept as a 'cul de sac template for estate design' (actually an earlier quote from Pascoe).

Figure 4.6   Diagram from the police Secured by Design literature (undated circa 1994)

It is this aspect of design guidance that Hillier was attacking when *Building Design* reported that a 'New report challenges conventional thinking on designing out crime' under a headline in inch high letters proclaiming the 'End of the road for the cul-de-sac' (Fairs, 1998). The article went on to say that 'They found that cul-de-sac areas – long advocated by the police and others in design guides as offering greater security – were highly vulnerable to burglary, as were other non-linear arrangements.' While it is true that the quote indicates that 'Linear streets with buildings along both sides emerged as the safest possible urban layout' it is clear that the principal target is the cul-de-sac planning of typical private developer housing.

Hillier and Shu set out their views on the cul-de-sac and crime in a paper 'Crime and urban layout: the need for evidence' (Hillier and Shu, 2000). They focus most attention on burglary. The study is based on residential areas in three English towns. In total the areas chosen contained 3500 houses.

The basis of their analysis is to use a technique called Space Syntax (for more information see www.spacesyntaxlaboratory.org). The movement spaces within the three residential areas were plotted as axial lines representing maximum sight lines through each space and producing a network of crossing lines overlaying each of the study areas. This was done for all through roads, cul-de-sac carriageways and footpaths. Crimes were plotted on this network of lines at the points from which entry was gained by burglars (front door off a street, back garden gate from a rear footpath, etc.).

Although there are more detailed aspects of their analysis, the general findings can be summarised as follows. The risk for each line in the analysis is calculated as a ratio of crimes per number of entry points along that line. The safest movement space was found to be a through carriageway with houses lining both sides of the street. The authors use the word 'constituted' to mean that at least 75% of the road is lined with house frontages. Footpaths, particularly rear dead-end footpaths providing access to back gardens, are the most prone to burglary in terms of rate of burglary per point of access (entry). Cul-de-sac carriageways are somewhere in between.

These findings are clearly of great interest. The idea that access from the rear by footpath is a high risk is obviously not new and seems to be a generally expected and accepted fact. What is new is the difference between through-streets and cul-de-sac carriageways. Overall the risk rates indicate that the risk for cul-de-sacs (1 burglary per 31 potential points of entry) is more than twice that for through roads (1 in 76).

Not only is this idea contrary to more generally held ideas about cul-de-sac developments – that they tend to keep out strangers and promote a more shared responsibility among neighbours for keeping an eye on each other's property – but it appears to run counter to another study of two suburban municipalities near Vancouver, BC (Beavon et al, 1994).

In this study the street patterns were analysed into a series of street segments, each representing the length of street between every street junction. Although they appear to have had difficulty allowing for the effects of different levels of traffic, the existence of different kinds of business on main streets, and the number and value of properties or length of each street segment, they did generate a very convincing graph showing a clear relationship between the amount of crime on each segment and the number of turnings in/out of it. The graph (Figure 4.7) shows that the street segments with the fewest turnings have the least crime. That appears to be saying that dead-end streets, which by definition have the fewest turnings, have the least crime. To help clarify, a typical street in a conventional grid pattern has six turnings, three turnings at each end (left, right and straight on) A conventional cul-de-sac as a side turning off another street might have just two turnings (left and right).

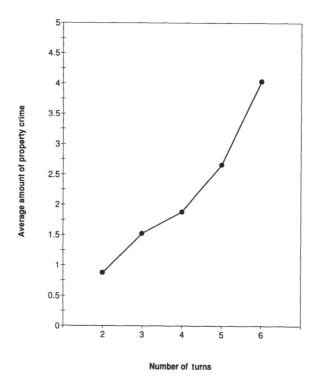

Figure 4.7   Graph from Beavon et al (1984) showing relationship between the amount of crime on each street segment and the number of street segments to which it is joined (turnings)

In support of this Canadian study Rengart and Hakim obtained evidence from the 1993 Greenwich study which graduated a hierarchy of roads in terms of busyness that underlines the safety of cul-de-sacs. It is clear from their table 3-3 (see Table 4.2) that the busier the street the great the risk of burglary (Rengart and Hakim, 1998: 48). However, the key difference between the cul-de-sac and the quiet residential road is small suggesting that the difference between through-roads and cul-de-sacs is trivial compared with some other factors influencing burglary. It also adds weight to the earlier observation that busily trafficked roads have increased risks for burglary.

Table 4.2   Burglary and type of street – from Rengart and Hakim (1998)

Type of street	Number of houses	Percentage burgled
Cul-de-sac	603	11.6
Quiet residential street	1,310	12.7
Commercial street	147	17.7
Busy residential street	202	21.3
Back road/local traffic	109	23.9

What are we to make of the cul-de-sac issue? Is Hillier right to condemn the cul-de-sac to a history of 20th century planning errors? As we have seen from the Northampton analysis, there is some advantage in having through movement of traffic through housing areas, as long as it is only very light movement. This is borne out by Rengart and Hakim's table above. However, is there sufficient evidence to say that cul-de-sacs have a negative effect on crime (i.e. makes burglary more likely)?

In the reworked analysis of the Northampton 1987 data it was decided to test Hillier and Shu's contentions. Lines 8 and 9 of Figures 4.3 and 4.4 assess the effect on burglary of Layout Areas with grid street patterns and cul-de-sac systems. If we combine the results of the two analyses we obtain the results summarised in Table 4.3. It shows quite surprisingly a similar paradox as with the question in line 7 on accessibility from main roads. The conditions that suit electrical goods burglary are completely different from those that suit cash and jewellery burglary.

Table 4.3   Grid street pattern compared with cul-de-sac road systems

Type of road	Electrical goods	Cash and jewellery
8. Grid streets (with some short cul-de-sacs)	LOW CRIME	HIGH CRIME
9. Cul-de-sac road systems	HIGH CRIME	LOW CRIME

If these contradictory results can be seen as rationally based on the difference in the two crimes then it would make nonsense to recommend grid streets over cul-de-sacs. Well, it can be seen as a rational result. If burglars want to avoid being seen escaping with bulkier suspicious items of electrical goods, then they would prefer cul-de-sacs (especially as these road patterns are in areas with a maze of footpaths to ideal escape routes). On the other hand the cash and jewellery burglary is much more likely to choose accessible through-streets with plenty of houses to consider for possible targets.

Faced with all this evidence it seems very clear to this author that no recommendation can be made to favour the through street at the expense of the cul-de-sac, or vice versa. It seems that from the burglary point of view, it does not matter whether a house is in a through-street or a cul-de-sac. The safety of a house and an area as a whole is going to be determined (influenced) by other design and layout factors.

Footpath systems

A much better explanation for the vulnerability of cul-de-sac systems is clear from the part of the analysis shown in lines 11–13, all of which deal with footpaths. All three lines in Figure 4.3 show very high levels of crime. From the electrical goods burglar's point of view the footpaths provide just that covert escape route that is essential for carrying off bulkier items. It seems quite clear that avoiding this kind of weakness in design and layout must be avoided if this more brazen form of burglary is to be stopped.

The problem with the Hillier and Shu study is that their space syntax techniques, which are able to predict the relative amount of normal movement along the axial lines of their analysis, does not take account of how burglars escape from the crime scene. On the other hand, the method used by Beavon et al, although it does not explicitly address the issue of escape, does replicate the number of options for escape in that it counts the number of turns out of each segment. The more turns would suggest more opportunity for escape, which fits the graph in Figure 4.7 very well. It is also clear from their literature review that Beavon et al are very much aware of the issue of cul-de-sacs and footpaths. They cite a Canadian case study in which the closure of footpaths leading from a cul-de-sac dramatically reduced crime in a residential neighbourhood (Beavon et al, 1994; Sheard, 1991).

It seems that we can confidently conclude that:

To reduce risk of electrical goods burglary, housing layouts should avoid road access systems that rely on a network of separate footpaths to provide adequate linkage to local facilities, transport, open space and other residential areas. It is better to use the street network for most pedestrian movement.

Terraces or detached and semi-detached

Before moving on, it seems worth asking the question about terraced houses versus detached houses. This was raised strongly as an issue in the early study by Winchester and Jackson who were able to generate hugely different risk rates for burglary between detached and terraced housing. Their overall figure for detached houses was 1 in 31 to 1 in 209 for a semi-detached house or short terrace, and for long terraces their figure was very low risk of 1 in 534 – a level that most of us would regard as a virtually crime-free status (Winchester and Jackson, 1982: table C1).

The analysis in lines 14 and 15 of Figures 4.3 and 4.4 is not so absolute as Winchester and Jackson's but compares layouts that are predominantly of terraced forms (typically 4 in a row but some much longer) and those that were predominantly detached or semi-detached. From this generalised comparison the average crime rates for electrical goods burglaries are little different from the overall average. However, there is some difference for cash and jewellery which seems to suggest that cash and jewellery burglary is more likely to occur in detached and semi-detached housing. This could be influenced by the fact that detached housing is often in higher income areas. More likely this is due to the factor discussed below, that cash and jewellery burglary relies mainly on gaining access to the back of the house by going around the side.

Relation of houses to streets

In *Crime Free Housing* the general value of planning housing to face onto the street was seen as a general principle for safe residential streets (not only burglary but also car crime and theft from around the house). It is a principle that Hillier and Shu came to recognise in their analysis; they gave it the name of 'constituted', which refers to streets 'with more than 75 per cent of dwelling front entrances on both sides' (Hillier and Shu, 2000: 232).

In terms of the reworked analysis in Figures 4.3 and 4.4, there is relatively little direct evidence to show that this principle of 'streets overlooked by houses along both sides' (line 16) differentiates between high and low crime layouts. This is because all but seven layouts have this characteristic, which is spread across the whole range of Layout Areas. However, if we look at the Layout Areas where houses do not face the street (lines 17–19) there is a clear differentiation. Where:

17. Many houses face across greens and/or face onto greens or footpaths; or

18. Houses sometimes face the back of other houses; or

19. Not all streets are overlooked by houses;

there is clear evidence that there is much more electrical goods burglary. This does not apply to cash and jewellery that has an average for these lines of the analysis much the same as the average for the crime:

In the interests of preventing electrical goods burglary, it is strongly recommended that houses should be laid out facing each other across a street.

This is done primarily to encourage surveillance from neighbouring houses and so reduce the willingness of burglars to approach a target house.

Informality in housing layout

In revisiting this analysis it was noticed that many of the layouts suffering from high levels of electrical goods burglary (particularly the top three Layout Areas at risk from electrical goods burglary 28, 33 and 24) were modern developer housing with cul-de-sac road layouts and housing facing the street. Part of this could be explained by the fact that these developments were connected to footpath networks, but it might have been expected that because houses faced the street this might give some protection. Looking in more detail at these layouts, although the streets are lined with houses, the houses are planned informally with varying set backs and at different angles, particularly to follow around the bends in the road and around the ends of cul-de-sacs. It seemed reasonable to believe that the informality of these layouts might make the street more 'welcoming' to burglars searching for targets and ultimately trying to escape. The informality of the plan, coupled with a tendency for trees and shrubs to be planted on the front open-plan gardens, gives the effect of fewer houses overlooking the street at any particular point.

The rather unscientific description given to these layouts was 'Higgledy-piggledy streets' as shown in line 20 of Figures 4.3 and 4.4, and illustrated in Figure 4.8. Comparing line 20 in both figures there is a clear indication that 'higgledy-pigglediness' is closely associated with electrical goods burglary but not cash and jewellery, which is little different from the overall average for that crime (6.5 compared with 6.2).

Figure 4.8   A map illustrating Layout Area 24 with the highest rate of electrical burglary

This finding could be dismissed as just a silly description of modern developer housing, but it has been included here because it points the way to several weaknesses in this informal approach to planning housing layout. It seems likely that informal layouts make it more difficult to effectively observe the street from the houses, and because these layouts create so many awkward junctions it is more difficult to create well defended boundaries around back gardens. These implications are discussed further below in more detail, but it is worth noting that identifying the problem of informality of layout resonates well with current thinking on urban design which emphasises the importance of creating streets with more ordered enclosure and continuity of frontages, to encourage a sense of place making.[1]

It may be helpful in the reduction of electrical goods burglary if:

Designers should take advantage of the principle of more enclosure and continuity of frontages to create a more ordered layout plan.

Front gardens

There are a number of aspects of front gardens worth considering in relation to burglary risk. The first is the presence of foliage screening the view of the front door and side access to a house. Foliage was clearly identified in *Crime Free Housing* and continues to be included in the reworked data at line 21 of Figures 4.3 and 4.4. Technically there are problems in revisiting data on foliage in these streets fifteen years on from the original study. It is clear that planting continues to grow and in revisiting many of the Layout Areas, it is quite striking how much growth has taken place, in terms of evergreen hedges, trees and shrubs. However, memory is unreliable and no detailed survey records were made for the original study and so the current analysis has to rely on the original ratings on foliage and a limited number of photographs from that time.

The findings are as clear as before: there is a clear difference between the two kinds of burglary. Obscuring the front door and any side access to the rear garden is clearly helpful to cash and jewellery burglars whereas it plays no part in vulnerability to electrical goods burglary. Clearly, to reduce the risk of cash and jewellery burglary, layout design needs to discourage planting in front of and around the door and side access that might obscure surveillance from the street and neighbouring houses. This is a finding well supported elsewhere in research on burglary. For example, Palmer et al found that 70.9% of the 86 burglars replying to their questionnaire chose 'thick vegetation around the house' as their best option when choosing a target house (Palmer et al, 2002). Similar findings emerge from Nee and Taylor's interviews of Irish burglars, 55% of whom rate the lack of visibility by passers-by and the presence of vegetation as cover as very important (Nee and Taylor, 1988).

We can conclude that:

Reduced visibility of the front door and any side access to a house is a major reason for cash and jewellery burglary to occur. Care must be taken to prevent the growth of mature foliage to obscure this view – perhaps by minimising front garden space and paving the area between doors/side access and the street.

It may seem strange that while foliage in front of front doors etc. encourages cash and jewellery burglary it appears to discourage electrical goods burglary, as the distribution on line 21 in Figure 4.3 suggests. This difference for electrical goods may just be an artefact of the sample of Layout Areas in the study, reflecting that there is a difference in the distribution of the two types of burglary. For example, we know that many of the houses in the new town area of Northampton which have high levels of electrical goods burglary have very minimal front gardens with little planting. The reason for their vulnerability to burglary is that their back gardens have gates with little security – often left open.

---

1. 'Continuity and enclosure' is one of the objectives of urban design set out in *By Design*, a joint publication by the government and CABE (Commission for Architecture and the Built Environment (DETR/CABE, 2000).

Another possibility may be seen more clearly in the next line of the analysis (line 22) that examines the effect on burglary of having a front garden defined by boundary fences, walls or hedges. In *Crime Free Housing* it was speculated that the use of an enclosed front garden might hinder an escaping burglar carrying goods. If he had to leave the house from the front, he would have to carry the goods to a front gateway to reach the street and might be more likely to draw attention to himself. Perhaps such burglars prefer more open fronts if their getaway is from the front of the house.

Changing fashions in front garden design seem to demand some kind of assessment of how deep private space in front of the house should be. In the earlier book the recommendation, from Alice Coleman, that houses should have gardens with 3–5 metres in front of the house was tested against the Northampton layouts in line 23 of the analysis (Coleman, 1987). Interestingly, for both kinds of crime the average crime risk of houses with this specification are much the same as the overall averages. It would seem that we can safely conclude that this requirement for a 3–5 metre garden does not seem relevant to burglary control.

So, what should be recommended? Designers must decide on front garden depth on the basis of other considerations than just burglary control, but from the crime point of view, some enclosure of a front garden may help reduce electrical goods burglary but it risks acquiring mature planting of small trees, shrubs and hedges that can obscure surveillance of the fronts of houses, especially the front door or side gates.

Perhaps the recent trend to create only small private strips in front of houses is the best strategy. The use of low walls and fences may be more necessary when the street is relatively busy. Certainly the idea of putting down generous areas of paving in front of front doors and side gates would go a long way to avoiding later excessive growth of garden planting.

Back gardens

The idea of a secure back garden or yard was seen as an important part of the recommendations in *Crime Free Housing* to prevent burglary. The rationale for this view is based on the common finding that many illegal entries to houses are via rear ground floor doors and windows. Checking this fact, however, reveals wide variations. In our original study of 1982 data the entry points were nearly all at the rear. Rear ground floor windows were the first choice, rear doors the next. Front doors and windows were also used to gain access but this was a small proportion (see Table 4.4).

This picture is rather different from the data produced by Budd (1999) who indicated that the proportion of front and rear entries is split roughly 50/50. However, Budd points out that many of the front entries apply to flats and in her more detailed breakdown for houses (terraced or otherwise) the proportion of rear entries is 55%. Interestingly, this is a remarkably similar figure to that in Maguire's early work on burglary of 54.5% rear entry (Maguire, 1982: table A11). The above are actual crime data. It is even more interesting to see that the rear entry is preferred by burglars. Palmer et al, in a questionnaire to 88 burglars, found that 53.5% of them listed a ground floor rear window as their best option for entry and 43.0% listed the back door as their best option (Palmer, Holmes and Hollin, 2002).

Table 4.4 Points of entry to houses from 1982 data from Harrow (previously unpublished)

Location			Percentage of crimes		
			Luxury goods N=39	Electrical goods N=102	Cash and jewellery N=111
Rear	Window	Ground floor	38	26	30
		Upper floors	10	4	12
	Door	Ground floor	23	21	27
		First floor	–	–	1
Side	Window	Ground floor	5	5	3
		First floor	3	–	–
	Door	Ground floor	3	2	2
Front	Window	Ground floor	3	10	3
	Door	Ground floor	3	14	14
	Garage		–	1	–
Skylight			3	–	–
Exact location of point of entry unknown			10	17	12
			100	100	100

Several researchers have raised the issue of access around the side of the house to the rear as a factor in increased burglary risk. It was one of the variables in Winchester and Jackson's risk index (Winchester and Jackson, 1982). It was also proposed as a pattern for prevention in Poyner (1983: pattern 4.7). More recently, Evans and Fletcher found this to be one of the few of their environmental criteria to have a significant association with residential burglary. They found that 55% of their sample of burgled houses had visible access front to rear on the left-hand side compared with 39% of non-burgled houses. For some curious reason this did not work for the right-hand side of the house. No doubt this must be something to do with their sample and not that burglars tend to be left-handed (Evans and Fletcher, 1998: table 4).

Turning to the data in Figures 4.3 and 4.4 there is an attempt to update the original data about back garden security. Although there is an attempt to simplify the data in line with the other elements in the analysis, it was difficult to check the status of side access (line 24) since there is some evidence of changes taking place (discussed in Chapter 7 'Fifteen years on'). The original analysis was based on a very rough judgement of side access – essentially, if it was possible to see through to the back. However, during this follow-up exercise it was clear that some gaps had been closed with light wrought iron or flimsy timber gates that clearly have no locks or secure bolts and so this new analysis tends to classify more areas as accessible. It is also true that rear gates may equally be insecure and therefore judgements about rear access to gardens are simply based on whether or not there are gates to rear paths or driveways etc. (even though we know that burglars can enter rear gardens and yards by climbing over fences and in some cases gaining access through damaged and broken-down fencing).

The two types of burglary produce different findings. The cash and jewellery burglars seem to benefit most where there is side access to the rear (line 24). It is also an apparent advantage to them to have longer/large back gardens (line 26), perhaps to provide more cover when attempting to force access to back doors or windows. This very much supports the notion that cash and jewellery burglary is primarily targeted from the front of the house. Indeed, it might be argued that it is the preferred form of burglary for the traditional street setting. This fits the fact that it tends to occur in the older streets built in the first half of the twentieth century.

The key issue here seems to be that:

Side access to the rear garden of the house should be fitted with a robust lockable gate. The more visible this point is to the street and neighbouring houses the better. For this reason it is best not recessed behind the general line of the house frontages.

Electrical goods burglary is much more common in the younger housing, with more informal layouts (higgledy-piggledy) and layouts where the convention of houses facing across the street was abandoned. Here the opportunities for burglary are much more open and varied. The point of access to the back gardens appears to be as much from the rear (by climbing or rear gate access as from any side access.

A further characteristic of layouts that relates to accessibility of rear gardens by climbing over fences etc. is line 28, which examines the effect of protecting rear gardens by planning them back-to-back. Previous authors, notably Coleman (1987), have suggested that one strong feature of 1930s-style developer housing is that they are generally designed with gardens backing onto each other from different streets. This seems to provide an obvious mutual protection because any criminal gaining access by climbing a back fence would be doubly at risk of being spotted by owners of the neighbouring gardens.

Curiously, this idea had not been tested in the first book, but when included in this analysis in line 28, it turned out to be a very effective clue to the nature of access for these different types of burglary. Indeed from Figures 4.3 and 4.4 it is clear that, while this back garden arrangement is of little relevance to cash and jewellery burglary, the housing Layout Areas that suffer heavily from electrical goods burglary are not protected by this common pattern. Although we do not have direct information about these burglaries, it would appear that many of the burglaries where the aim is to steal bulkier items gain access via rear garden walls and fences.

Creating layouts in which gardens are planned back to back or and side by side appears to be an effective means of largely eliminating access from the rear of the house

One final point that ties in with this route of entry is the effect of long/large back gardens on electrical goods burglary (line 26). While larger gardens seem to help cash and jewellery burglars to maintain cover, having gained access around the side of the house, they may provide a disincentive to burglars considering climbing fences to enter a rear garden. There must be more risk to the intending burglar to climb into a garden full of trees and plants. He might have miscalculated and find that someone is in the house or that a neighbour sees him gaining access. Better for a rear entry to choose a small empty garden that can be easily checked before entry is attempted. The small gardens of modern houses are much more suited to this form of entry.

Key points for designing out burglary

Having worked through all the aspects of the analysis in Figures 4.3 and 4.4 it becomes clear that the two kinds of burglary need different design approaches to effectively eliminate the risk (or at least make it as small as possible). Indeed further reflection about the two kinds of burglary suggests that they are different responses to two broadly different kinds of built environment.

Electrical goods burglary takes place in the more vulnerable layouts where houses do not necessarily face across the street and where there are many footpath escape routes. These situations enable burglars to gain access from the front or back gardens not only through recognised entry points but also over vulnerable fences etc., particularly where gardens do not back onto other gardens but open areas or edges of developments and where there are footpaths along side or back fences. In these kinds of layouts there is not much point in burglars limiting what they take to small valuable and easily concealed items; they will feel able to take more.

Cash and jewellery burglary is much more constrained. It seems to take place most often in more conventional streets with access at the side of the house but not otherwise to the back garden. This kind of burglary is less risky in these types of layout than trying to take away larger items. In this kind of layout the emphasis for prevention is more on keeping a watchful eye on the front door and side access to a house. It relies mostly on preventing access to the back via the side access, making sure the front door and side gates are fully overseen from the street and neighbouring houses.

A summary of the recommendations is discussed under a 'Strategy to avoid house burglary' in Chapter 9.

One of most innovative aspects of *Crime Free Housing* was to identify the issue of vehicle crime as one of layout design. Although the main approach to reducing car crime has been to improve car security, a notable success of the 1990s, there can be little doubt from the research in Harrow and Northampton that the design of the residential environment can have a huge effect on the levels of vehicle crime.

The first data to emerge from the research that led to the conclusions in *Crime Free Housing* was from the 1982 police data for both Harrow and Northampton. The following Table 5.1 is reconstructed from an original unpublished project report and includes data on the theft of components (parts) as well as theft of cars and the theft of property from inside cars.

Table 5.1 Locations of residential car crimes in Harrow and Northampton (1982 data)

Location	Harrow			Northampton		
Actual numbers in samples	theft of	property	parts	theft of	property	parts
Garage	1	3	–	2	1	–
Driveway/hardstanding in front	5	13	6	2	4	2
Back alleyways	1	2	–	–	1	–
Parking areas/bays	2	1	–	9	17	2
Street outside house	54	42	5	31	15	1
Location category not known	39	23	6	19	10	3
TOTALS	102	84	17	63	48	8

Source: Poyner, Helson and Webb (1985)

This table is highly informative. It is clear that most of the residential car crime occurs to cars parked in the street, with the additional warning from the Northampton data that cars are also at risk in communal parking bays. Of course, the actual risks and recorded crime levels will depend on how any particular residential area is designed. No doubt, if more cars were kept in back alleyways this would increase the amount of theft from that kind of location. Nevertheless, it is relatively easy to believe from this data that cars are less likely to be the target of crime if they are parked on private driveways in front of houses rather than in the street. Indeed, the difference in the figures between levels of crime in the street and on private driveways is much greater than any reduction in crime so far from improved car security (see also Table 5.2).

From a theoretical point of view there seems to be evidence here for Newman's defensible space theory. It is not enough to claim that the reason behind this pattern of crime is the amount of supervision or surveillance that can be given to a car parked in front of a house or in the street. There seems to be something more than just surveillance. Parking on land actually belonging to the house seems to confer an additional protective effect. This would be what Newman called 'territoriality'. There are no physical barriers to gaining access to parked cars, just nominal or symbolic boundaries (Newman, 1973: chapter 3).

In more recent British Crime Surveys a limited amount of information has been recorded about the location of car crimes. The exact meaning of the categories is unclear but the figures for all vehicle theft at home in 2000 (*of* vehicles, *from* and attempts) amount to 64% of all vehicle theft, of which

2% was from private space, 26% from semi-public space and 36% from the street. Presumably the researchers use the 'semi-public' category, following Oscar Newman's terminology, to mean parking space that does not belong to individual houses (private) but is not part of the public street. This must include shared parking bays, courts and alleys in housing developments (Kershaw et al, 2000: table A5.6). These BCS statistics are highly supportive of the data in Table 5.1.

The 1987 data from north-east Northampton

To explore this issue of parking and car crime further, 1987 data collected from the police for north-east Northampton was mapped and analysed in a similar method to that for burglary. As in the case of burglary only the two largest categories were included – theft of cars and theft of property from the inside of cars.

Unlike burglary, the locations of car crime are much less clearly recorded in the police record. For example, it may not be clear where the car might have been parked in a particular street or if it was parked in a garage court etc. This is reflected in the largish numbers in the last line of Table 5.1. A major advantage of the methodology used in this research is that precise information about the location of each incident is not absolutely necessary as long as we know to which Layout Area it belongs. The analysis is merely concerned with the levels of crime in different kinds of layout design and correlating the two. In this way all the relevant crime data can be used in the analysis.

The maps in Figures 5.1 and 5.2 show the distribution of car crimes in the 38 Layout Areas. Unlike the contrast between the two types of burglary, these two maps are much more similar. The outer suburbs are much more heavily targeted for both types of car crime than the areas closer to the town centre. Some Layout Areas, particularly for thefts *of* cars, are almost crime free (e.g. Areas 10, 11, 12 and 14). Although a general view of the map might lead some with a conventional view of criminology to claim that the distribution is largely due to the pattern of tenure at the time, it is difficult to rely on a social class argument when adjacent Layouts Areas have hugely contrasting

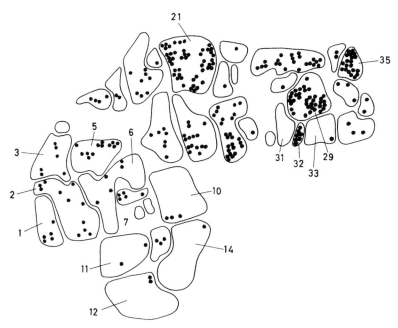

Figure 5.1   Distribution of thefts of cars in north-east Northampton (1987 data)

levels of crime. If income or other social factors influenced crime, why should 'theft *of* cars' not be spread more evenly across a group of Layout Areas such as 29, 31, 32 and 33. After all they are only a few metres from each other and they are linked by footpaths. An offender living in any one of these areas can easily move between them.

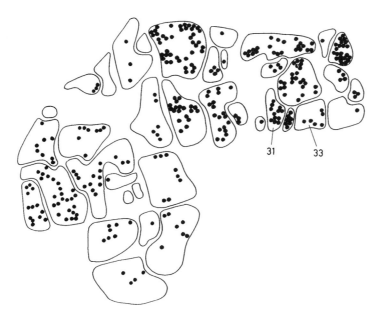

Figure 5.2   Distribution of theft of property from inside cars in north-east Northampton (1987 data)

The analysis is in a similar form to that for burglary, but the range of issues covered is fewer, largely because the pattern behind these crimes is easier to understand. The analysis is presented in Figures 5.3 and 5.4, which are included at the end of this chapter.

Minimising car theft

Taking Figure 5.3 theft *of* cars first, the first three lines of the analysis look at the relation between income levels in the different Layout Areas and car theft. It is interesting that there is a much stronger relationship here than for either of the burglary types. As will be seen from the rest of the analysis this is best explained by design than by social deprivation. However, there is a link. The lower-income Layout Areas tend to be designed to much lower standards of parking provision. This is not so much in terms of the amount of parking but the extent to which residents are able to park their cars close to their houses. It is the better off middle-class housing that has space for parking in front or to the side of houses, whereas it is the lower-income housing where parking is in communal parking bays often to the side or rear of terraced housing. So, in one sense those living in lower-income housing are more socially deprived not just in the familiar socio-economic sense but also in terms of the provision for safe car parking.

Street patterns

Since the issue of street pattern has been raised in the previous chapter, it seemed worth considering the same questions for car crime. The issue of a drive-through route (line 6) seems unimportant to the theft *of* cars as it averages the same as the overall rate for this crime. However, there are differences between grid streets and cul-de-sac road systems (lines 8 and 9). Grid street patterns appear to have less car theft than cul-de-sacs, although it has to be said that quite a number of cul-de-sac systems have little car theft (see line 9). The average for grid streets is a theft rate of 11.6/1000, well below the average of 17.1.

Hillier and Shu make a brief reference to car crime in their paper on through-streets versus cul-de-sacs (Hillier and Shu, 2000: 241). They claim a similar but weaker finding for car crime as they did for burglary – that it is safer to park in a through-street than a cul-de-sac. If they are right, then there is agreement here, at least for the theft *of* cars. However, one wonders how relevant their methodology is when they still base their calculation of car crime rate on the number of entry points to a line. A rate of crime per entry points makes sense for burglary which by definition requires some entry point, but it does not make sense for car crime that can take place in spaces with no points of entry.

However, the conclusion from the above is that:

Grid street patterns appear to be less at risk from thefts of cars than cul-de-sac patterns.

Presumably the argument for this is that through movement of light traffic and pedestrians increases the risk of potential offenders being seen attempting to enter and drive away a vehicle. The scientific problem is to decide how important this is in relation to other factors below that tend to be more common in grid street designs – the fact that houses are more likely to face onto the street and that street parking and the existence of private driveways are more common in these types of street.

Footpath systems

It might be argued that some of the increased risk from the cul-de-sac forms comes from the link with footpaths systems (lines 11, 12 and 13). Indeed the average crime rates for these lines in the analysis are well above the overall average of 17.1 and do seem to imply that cars are easier to steal in an environment that is easily penetrated on foot. This suggests that an important part of the *modus operandi* is to wander around a neighbourhood looking for vulnerable and suitable cars to steal (see also Case Study 2 in Chapter 8). This would also explain why so much of the car theft is focused on the outer suburban area of eastern Northampton where planners had created a completely segregated network of footpaths by which potential car thieves can roam freely, gaining access to areas in which cars are generally parked in public and semi-public spaces.

Networks of segregated footpaths appear to increase the risk of car theft.

Arrangements for parking to avoid thefts of cars

Looking at lines 16 to 22 in the analysis, the first clear division between safer and least safe is when houses are designed to face onto the street. Line 16 of the analysis shows that the highest car theft rates are found where houses do not face onto the street. This is also directly associated with layouts in which parking is mainly in semi-private parking bays or courts (lines 19 and 20).

To see the pattern as a whole, it is useful to extract the relevant data from Table 5.3, so that the average crime rates for the various forms of parking provision can be seen and compared more easily, as follows:

17. On private driveways in front/at the side	9.1
21. Garages next to house	10.1
18. Parking in streets overlooked by houses	13.5
---17.1 average rate	
22. Garage courts or alleyways (at rear of houses)	22.9
19. Shared parking bays or courts in front of houses	33.9
20. Shared parking unsupervised from houses	40.3

The conclusion from this tabulation needs little explanation. It means that in this analysis, Layout Areas where cars are parked predominantly on private driveways have a much lower average rate of car theft. A similar level is found in layouts where garages are located at the side of the house. Even where there is a good deal of on-street parking the theft level is still well below average. However, where a Layout Area is designed predominantly with parking in communal bays, the levels of crime soar to over twice the average rate, whether the parking bays are in front of the houses or not.

Conclusions about designing out car theft

The conclusions about layout design and car theft appear to be very clear and direct. From the evidence of the Northampton study and earlier data from Harrow:

> *The safest place to park is off the street on private driveways in front (or possibly the side) of houses.*

> *Parking on the street is the safest alternative, and this will be safer on through streets (carrying light traffic).*

> *Housing with many footpath connections linking streets will encourage car thieves to target the area. Pedestrian movement should follow the general lines of vehicle movement.*

Although the evidence in the Northampton study suggests that parking in the street is almost as safe as parking on a private driveway, the analysis is clear that a private driveway is safer. It should also be remembered that the data in Table 5.1 and in the British Crime Survey suggest much more strongly that the street is less safe than private driveways. Recognising that this is an important issue for planners, it has to be said that it is not practical to expect precise quantification of the differences in risk between these various parking locations. Much depends on the detail of the layouts that are subjected to research. However, the principle of parking on private space attached to a house is the best guarantee of a car crime free residential area. (See also comments and photographs in Chapter 7 – 'Fifteen years on'.)

Minimising theft from inside cars

Although the mappings of the two types of car crime appear similar in Figures 5.1 and 5.2, closer examination of the two rank order lists in Figures 5.3 and 5.4 shows that there are some significant differences. For small Layout Areas these differences may appear large when only small numbers of crimes are involved, but there are several Layout Areas with major differences where the numbers of crimes are substantial. For example, Layout Areas 31, 33, 6 and 11 have low rates of car theft but higher levels of theft from cars. Layout Areas 17, 38 and 7 are examples of the reverse relationship. Although many of these differences may not be statistically significant it is clear that rather different reasons may be behind the two crime distributions.

Household income

The first curious difference is that while the middle-income areas seemed to be protected from car theft (it was assumed this was because they lived in housing better provided with car parking on private driveways) their advantage disappears for the crime of thefts *from* cars. Instead of a crime level of less than half the average for theft of cars, they have only an average value for theft *from* cars. What this indicates is that the theft of property from inside cars is much more difficult to prevent through design and layout of Layout Areas.

Street patterns and footpaths

This point about theft *from* cars is reflected in the data for grid and cul-de-sac street patterns. There is still the same general relationship that grid layouts are safer but the difference is not quite so strong.

The evidence for involvement of footpath networks is also much the same for both types of car crime. Although one might expect the footpath networks to aid the escape from a scene of theft *from* cars, it does not appear to add to the risk over that for car theft.

Locations for parking

The array in Figure 5.4 for lines 16 to 22 is very similar to that for theft *of* cars but perhaps a little less tidy. The reason for this seems to be the fact that parking on driveways is not quite so safe for theft *from* cars as it is against the theft *of* cars. It is interesting to see that this is confirmed in the data in Table 5.1, which shows a little more crime of property theft occurring on private driveways.

This reason why the theft *of* cars from driveways is less likely than the thefts *from* cars is because efforts to start a car parked on a private driveway are bound to risk being seen or heard from the house. The taking of property *from* the car may be much easier and less risky. The same applies to components. One case from the early studies in Harrow which illustrates the idea of the relative ease of theft was the reported removal of hub caps of a classic Rolls-Royce car parked on a driveway overnight.

It is interesting that Sallybanks and Thomas report the increase in theft of components from cars emerging from recent findings in the British Crime Survey (Sallybanks and Thomas, 2000). Apart from the implied message that car security improvements may be causing some displacement of theft to external parts of cars, these observations suggest that the category of theft *from* cars is likely to remain a more persistent problem than the theft *of* cars.

The conclusion that seems necessary from this analysis is that the principles for prevention are the same for the two kinds of car crime, but because theft *from* cars is likely to be more difficult to eradicate, it only adds weight to the argument that parking provision on private land is the most desirable. Indeed, it suggests that more care is needed to find effective ways of protecting parking areas. It would be useful to experiment and monitor the effect of design on theft *from* cars. Perhaps the use of more gates and the careful positioning of windows and doors would add to any territorial advantage or improved surveillance of parking. Street parking, while safer than many of the parking arrangements of many housing developments of the past, must be seen as still vulnerable. This is only made worse by the ever greater demand for parking. The issues are discussed again in Chapter 7 and Case Study 2 in Chapter 8.

Effect of improving car security

It is now generally accepted that one of the great successes of crime prevention policy, started in the mid-1980s and pressed home through the 1990s, is the improvement in security specifications for motor cars. Indeed, we have come a long way since the pioneering thinking about the idea of a crime-free car (Southall and Ekblom, 1985). The data emerging from the Home Office car theft index indicates clearly that newer cars are much less at risk of being stolen than older cars. The improvement in crime statistics is most evident in the drop in car theft in the recorded crime figures between 1991 and 2001 and in the number of attempts reported through the British Crime Surveys from 1995 (see Table 5.2).

Table 5.2 Comparison of motor vehicle crimes in both police recorded and BSC sources from 1991 to 2001

Police recorded crime	1991	1995	1997	1999/00	2000/01	2001/02	Max. drop
Theft of vehicle	581,901	502,280	399,208	364,270	328,037	316,404	46%
Theft from vehicle	913,276	813,094	710,333	669,232	629,651	655,127	28%
Vehicle interference	–	–	–	56,521	62,696	80,750	–
Crim. damage to veh.	–	–	–	374,218	378,903	419,757	–
Vehicle crime recorded	1,495,177	1,315,374	1,109,541	1,464,241	1,399,287	1,472,038	[2%]
BCS (000s)	1991	1995	1997	1999	2000	2001/02	
Theft of vehicles	519	510	378	336	344	330	36%
Theft from vehicles	2,412	2,542	2,200	1,849	1,742	1,560	39%
Attempts (of/from)	894	1,296	933	825	706	707	46%
Vehicle vandalism	1,677	1,825	1,609	1,594	1,582	1,579	13%
Total BSC vehicle crime	5,502	6,173	5120	4,604	4,374	4,176	32%

Based on tables 3.01 and 3.04 in *Crime in England and Wales 2001/2002* (Simmons et al, 2002)

The reduction in the theft of cars is regarded as largely due to technology such as the use of immobilisers with other aspects of technology such as remote locking and alarm systems having a supporting role. Theft from cars has also reduced and much of this is no doubt due to improved technology and the development of theft-proof car radios and disc players. Many manufacturers have made the removal of such items virtually impossible by integrating them into the car structure, rather than designing them as an easily removed component package.

With such an impact from improvements in car security it might be argued that the need for design and layout of housing to protect against car crime is greatly reduced. Part of the answer is to point out that car crime is still alive and well and certainly the parts of this report based on recent crime data show that it remains a significant part of the residential crime problem. See Chapter 7 and Case Studies 1 and 2 to appreciate the continued impact of car crime.

To take this matter further, it is helpful to look at the national crime figures in more detail. Even allowing for a continued trend in reducing car crime, there remains a very large amount of crime associated with cars that is not so easily dealt with by improving security technology. There are two quite different issues. When the early studies were done for this research into housing layout in the 1980s, the analysis of residential crime indicated that the ratio of thefts *of* cars to theft *from* cars was roughly equal (even though national statistics showed a ratio of about 2 to 1 theft *from/of*). However, since the arrival of the British Crime Survey in the early 1980s it has always reported a much higher level of theft *from* vehicles than theft *of* vehicles. The ratio is typically 5 to 1. On the face of it this suggests that thefts *from* cars is a much bigger problem than often believed.

On top of this issue of theft *from* cars, the issue of criminal damage is often overlooked in the research. This was due in part in the earlier work to the fact that there was much less criminal damage to cars in our analysis. At the time, it was not easy to check since national statistics did not separate criminal damage to vehicles. Now that they are published separately, it emerges that there is a large and increasing amount of criminal damage being done to vehicles. British Crime Survey figures for vehicle vandalism (see also Table 5.2 above) make it clear how major a problem it is and that it does not seem to be reducing to the same extent as the other two crimes.

The conclusion from all this seems to be that the crime of car stealing may be significantly reduced by improved security added to the car at the design and manufacturing stages, but there is a good deal of car crime that is less likely to be solved through technology. While cars are parked in residential settings, the conditions under which cars are kept seems to be highly linked to crime risk.

Figure 5.3 Analysis of design and layout factors for theft of cars

LAYOUT AREAS / CRIME RATES IN RANK ORDER	av. 17.1	31 0	33 2	22 4	14 4	12 5	10 5	6 5	28 6	11 24 6 7	3 10	26 10	1 11	34 11	2 12	16 12	15 14	36 16	38 19	5 17	19 13 20 7 19 23 24 27	27 25 21 32 29 35 31 41 43 50 66
Household income																						
1. Upper-income households	13.2			X						X						X	X	X		X	X	X X X X X
2. Middle-income households	7.7	X	X	X	X	X	X	X	X		X X X X X			X	X						
3. Lower-income households	31.6									X		X	X		X	X			X		X X X X X X	X X X X X
Through-streets and cul-de-sacs																						
6. Drive-through route	17.1			X		X	X				X X X X			X	X		X		X X X X X	X X X X
7. Direct turning off a main road	10.5		X		X	X	X	X		X	X X X			X	X	X	X		X X	X X X X
8. Grid streets (includes some short cul-de-sacs)	11.6				X	X		X			X					X					X	
9. Cul-de-sac road system (includes loop roads)	19.9	X	X	X	X		X		X	X	X	X	X	X	X	X	X	X	X	X	X X X X X	X X X X X
Footpath systems																						
10. Layouts with blind cul-de-sacs (no footpaths)	13.2			X								X				X				X	X X	X X
11. Cul-de-sac roads linked to footpath networks	25.4	X	X	X		X	X	X	X		X	X			X		X	X		X	X X X	X X X X
12. Pedestrian-only routes through the area	21.5	X	X		X	X	X	X			X	X			X		X	X		X	X X	X X X X
13. Pedestrian escape routes to unsupervised parking	25.3	X				X	X	X			X	X			X		X				X	X X X
Predominant house form																						
14. Terraced housing – mainly in rows of four or more	24.3	X		X	X	X	X	X	X		X X			X				X		X	X X	X X
15. Detached and semi-detached	9.5		X	X	X	X	X	X	X	X	X	X					X	X	X	X	X	
Relation of houses to parking																						
16. Houses facing onto street	10.2	X	X	X	X	X	X	X	X	X	X	X	X	X	X	X	X	X	X	X	X X X	X X X X X
17. On private driveways in front/at side of house	9.1	X	X	X	X	X	X	X	X	X	X	X	X	X	X	X	X	X	X	X	X X X	X X X
18. Parking in streets overlooked by houses	13.5				X				X	X	X	X	X				X		X		X	X X
19. Shared parking bays or courts in front of houses	33.9												X				X				X X X	X X X X X
20. Shared parking unsupervised from houses	40.3																X				X X X	X X X X X
21. Garages next to house	10.1	X	X	X	X	X	X	X	X	X	X	X		X	X		X	X		X	X X X X	X X X X X
22. Garage courts or alleyways (at rear of houses)	22.9	X				X	X	X	X	X	X	X		X				X		X X	X	X X
23. Density – over 30 per hectare	22.4	X	X						X	X	X	X	X	X	X	X	X	X	X	X	X X	X X X X X

47

Figure 5.4 Analysis of design and layout factors for theft from cars

LAYOUT AREAS →
CRIME RATES IN RANK ORDER →

Column rank order (top row / bottom row):

16	22	7	34	38	17	13	15	5	12		3	10	33	6	19	36	28	11	25	2	24		14	26	27	20	29	1	31	21	32	35
0	4	5	5	7	8	9	10	10			13	13	15	16	16	22	24	24	25	27			28	29	29	31	33	34	35	37	43	73

Row	av. 20.8
Household income	
1. Upper-income households	14.4
2. Middle-income households	21.7
3. Lower-income households	29.0
Through-streets and cul-de-sacs	
6. Drive-through route	17.8
7. Direct turning off a main road	17.7
8. Grid streets (includes some short cul-de-sacs)	17.1
9. Cul-de-sac road system (includes loop roads)	22.4
Footpath systems	
10. Layouts with blind cul-de-sacs (no footpaths)	11.0
11. Cul-de-sac roads linked to footpath networks	26.1
12. Pedestrian-only routes through the area	27.5
13. Pedestrian escape routes to unsupervised parking	26.1
Predominant house form	
14. Terraced housing – mainly in rows of four or more	25.0
15. Detached and semi-detached	14.1
Relation of houses to parking	
16. Houses facing onto street	16.2
17. On private driveways in front/at side of house	15.5
18. Parking in streets overlooked by houses	16.9
19. Shared parking bays or courts in front of houses	29.1
20. Shared parking unsupervised from houses	38.6
21. Garages next to house	14.3
22. Garage courts or alleyways (at rear of houses)	26.2
23. Density – over 30 per hectare	25.5

Theft and damage around the home

The idea of discussing car crime as a separate residential crime problem was new with *Crime Free Housing*. The studies of residential crime in Harrow and Northampton also drew attention to other crime associated with garden areas and the immediate surroundings to the home. The book discussed these in three short chapters on 'Theft from garages', 'Theft outside the house' and 'Criminal damage'. The material in these chapters remains unique in that no other researchers or practitioners seem to have taken a serious interest in this aspect of crime in low-rise housing development.

Although there are no apparent challenges from recent research, it seems necessary to re-present the findings on theft and damage because otherwise they seem likely to be overlooked in future thinking about housing design and layout. In doing so, some of the data has been reorganised to discuss motorcycle theft as a separate crime and the familiar analysis matrices include some of the additional factors introduced in Chapters 4 and 5.

Why has theft and damage been given little attention in housing design?

The problem in understanding theft and damage around the home is that it is relatively difficult to extract from any national statistics. Domestic burglary is recorded as a separate statistical category, and car crime is readily understood as a major crime problem in residential and non-residential settings. Some of the official categories of theft are potentially confusing from the design point of view. For example, a theft from a garage is classified as 'Burglary other' if the garage has no internal door connecting it to a house. If there is a connecting door the theft is a 'Burglary in a dwelling'. If the object that is stolen from a garage is a bicycle, then the crime category is a 'Theft of a pedal cycle'. While these categories are quite understandable from the crime statistical viewpoint they fail to draw attention to the common problem of garage insecurity.

Most of the theft from around the house is recorded as 'Other crime' and so is normally lost to public perception. Another category of recorded crime that relates to theft from around the house is the theft of bicycles. Again, no national figure is available but the studies of Harrow and Northampton with 1982 data revealed that about half of all bicycle thefts occur around the house. These thefts were of bicycles, often belonging to male children, left in front gardens, driveways, back gardens. They also included bicycles stolen from mostly unlocked garages. Table 6.1 provides a summary of these figures.

Table 6.1 Theft of bicycles in the analysis of 1982 data

Location of bicycle theft	Harrow	Northampton	Total
Theft from garages and sheds[1]	nk	nk	23
Theft outside the house – driveways and gardens	26	23	49
Theft of bicycles left in public places	25	40	65

[1]Data from unpublished report (Poyner, Helson and Webb, 1985)

A category that is officially recorded under motor vehicle crime is the theft of motorcycles. Because of the preoccupation with the serious problem of car crime, motorcycle crime has been neglected. It is clear that the options for storing motorcycles are somewhere in between the car and bicycle and because they can be parked in front and back gardens as well as in garages and sheds, they are considered here as a separate category of theft from around the house. It is perhaps worth noting that if the use of cars is to be discouraged as part of transport policy, there is a good case for crime prevention policy to reduce the risk of theft for both bicycles and motorcycles and so make them safer to own. Judging from the early 1982 data for Harrow and Northampton, more than twice as many motorcycle thefts were from residential areas as non-residential locations. It would appear to be a more serious crime problem than residential bicycle theft.

Finally, there is the issue of criminal damage. This will be a familiar problem on run-down public-sector housing estates, particularly around blocks of flats and communal facilities. While it is true that criminal damage is generally less serious in low-rise housing it is not until very recently that national statistics have recorded 'Criminal damage to a dwelling' as a separate crime category. This began with the 1998/1999 statistics (see police recorded crime in Simmonds et al, 2002). It is also interesting that recorded 'Criminal damage to a dwelling' has steadily increased since 1998/1999.

All these categories share a relatively low-profile image compared with burglary and vehicle crime, but when assembled together they amount to a substantial body of residential crime. Table 6.2 lists all those crimes of theft and damage that occur around the home and that are not included elsewhere in the report. The classification is based on the 1987 data from north-east Northampton, but where possible comparable data from the 1982 samples is also included.

In presenting data in such detail, it is always unfair to expect a reader to fully absorb the implications on a first read through. It may, therefore, be helpful to put this classification of crime into a broader context. Table 6.3 summarises the sizes of the residential crime groups to show the relative size of this group of theft and damage around the home compared with the other principal groups. Each of the three samples has a different base but in rough proportions burglary is only just over a quarter of residential crime. Car crime is over a third, while theft and damage around the home amounts to a quarter of residential crime. No doubt a more up-to-date study would show an increase in this group in line with the decreases in burglary and car crime in recent years. Viewed in this way, perhaps more attention should be given to this slice of the crime cake. Although the costs of burglary and vehicle crime may be more significant than much of the theft and damage around the home, the threat and nuisance it creates in everyday life must contribute to negative feelings and anxiety about the neighbourhoods in which people live.

Table 6.2   Theft and damage around the home

Type of crime	1982 Harrow N	1982 Harrow N/1000	1982 N'pton N	1982 N'pton N/1000	1987 N'pton N	1987 N'pton N/1000
Theft from outbuildings						
Thefts from garages					59	4.3
Thefts from garden sheds					36	2.6
Theft from garages and sheds	**44**	**2.6**	**18**	**3.2**	**95**	**6.9**
Theft outside the house:						
Bicycles (from gardens and driveways)	26	1.6	23	4.0	56	4.0
Milk, parcels, etc. taken from doorsteps[1]	–	–	11	1.9	25	1.8
Clothes from washing lines	5	0.3	19	3.3	25	1.8
Plants and garden ornaments stolen	16	1.0	9	1.6	17	1.2
Property taken from external meter boxes[2]	–	–	–	–	7	0.5
Other theft outside the house	4	0.2	3	0.5	27	1.9
Total theft outside the house	**51**	**3.1**	**65**	**11.3**	**157**	**11.2**
Theft of motorcycles	16	1.0	17	3.0	127	9.1
Theft of components from motorcycles	2	0.1	2	0.3	8	0.6
Total of motorcycle theft from around the home	**18**	**1.1**	**19**	**3.3**	**135**	**9.7**
Criminal damage in residential areas[3]						
Stones and other objects through windows					68	4.9
Windows broken by airgun pellets					6	0.4
Other smashed windows					23	1.6
Door glass broken					16	1.1
Doors/windows forced					11	0.8
Garden fences, walls and gates damaged					24	1.7
Following an argument					16	1.1
Internal damage to houses and garages					9	0.6
Other damage to outside of houses					11	0.8
Other damage not to house or garage					10	0.7
Total of damage around the home	**89**	**5.3**	**18**	**3.1**	**194**	**13.7**
TOTAL theft and damage around the home	**202**	**12.1**	**120**	**20.9**	**581**	**41.5**

[1]Not recorded at that time in the Metropolitan Police area

[2]This category was not used in 1982 analysis

[3]Different classifications are given for criminal damage in the 1982 and 1987 data. The reason is simply that the detail available in the 1987 data was less than in 1982 due to computerisation and the limitations created by the Data Protection Act.

Table 6.3   Summary of main groups of residential crime

Type of crime	1982 Harrow N/1000	1982 Harrow per cent	1982 N'pton N/1000	1982 N'pton per cent	1987 N'pton N/1000	1987 N'pton per cent
Total residential burglary	22.0	39%	24.6	28%	43.5	27%
Total vehicle crime (excluding motorcycles)	19.3	35%	32.1	38%	68.2	42%
Total theft and damage around the home	12.1	22%	20.9	25%	41.5	25%
Other residential crimes	2.2	4%	6.8	9%	7.3	5%
TOTALS	55.6	100% (N=927)	84.4	100% (N=486)	160.5	100% (N=2232)

Thefts from garages

Garages typically contain a wide variety of items that can be attractive to a thief. The earlier studies provided more detail than the 1987 data and showed that apart from bicycles, the most common item, a bewildering array of power tools, gardening tools and particularly power mowers, food from freezer cabinets and sports equipment were taken.

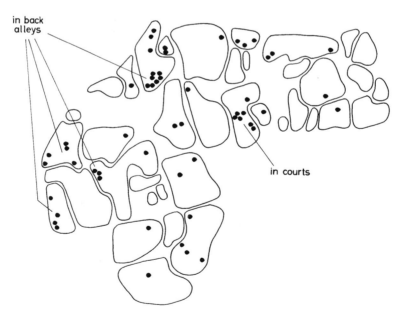

Figure 6.1   Map distribution of thefts from garages in the 1987 Northampton data

The details of the 59 thefts from garages in the 1987 Northampton data are set out in Figures 6.1 and 6.2. The map is the most helpful guide in that there are only eight Layout Areas with more than two thefts. The situations in which recorded thefts were reported are:

Area 1   Terraced houses having garages opening onto back alleyways

Area 3   As above

Area 6   As above

Area 14   Large houses set well back with detached garages

Area 17   Bungalow developments with garages opening onto back alleyways

Area 22   Some small garage courts

Area 25   Small groups of garages in unsupervised parking courts

Area 27   Isolated garages in unsupervised parking areas

From the above, there is clear evidence that in an area where there is a variety of arrangements in which garages are planned, there are clear problems for garages located other than next to the house. The matrix analysis in Figure 6.2 is not so clear as the annotated map. This is probably due to the small sample and the fact that some of the Layout Areas include different types of garage arrangement. For example, Area 17 has conventional garages at the side of many houses but also there are streets of bungalows with garages opening onto little-used back alleys. Smaller and more carefully defined Layout Areas would have produced a better analysis, but despite this methodological weakness the message about garage courts and back alleys is clear enough.

More out of curiosity than mainstream interest the matrix included lines 5–7 on the issue of grid and cul-de-sac layouts. The result shows a distinct difference. Cul-de-sac layouts have mostly zero theft from garages, even those streets linked to footpaths have generally low rates. However, the grid streets have higher rates (the two exceptions, Areas 2 and 7, have few garages from which to steal). There are two likely explanations for this. One is a *modus operandi* typical of the earlier Harrow data in which thieves prowl the streets, particularly in the more established or better off housing, looking for opportunities such as insecure garages. This is an after-dark activity unlike much house burglary which is more commonly a daytime pursuit. Another is that grid street layouts often have back alleyways with garages (e.g. Areas 1, 3 and 17).

Further clarification of the circumstances of these thefts, and the role of layout and security, came from early data in Harrow. Table 6.4 shows an analysis of 33 thefts from Harrow garages where clear information was recorded about the state of security of the garage at the time of the theft. There were no forced entries to garages close to the house. Of those thefts from garages away from the house, 7 out of 12 involved a physical break-in. Two conclusions emerge from this table. Firstly, the doors to garages next to the house do not require heavy security – they do not seem to be forced open – unlike garages away from the house that do require robust locking. The second conclusion is that the main problem is people leaving doors unlocked (several were left open). The solution to this is not entirely clear, but some comments in earlier records suggest that quite often doors are left unlocked because of difficulties in properly closing doors or because of damaged locks.

Figure 6.2 Analysis of design and layout factors for theft from garages

LAYOUT AREA — CRIME RATES IN RANK ORDER →	av. 3.5	38	36	35	34	32	31	28	26	24	15	13	7	2	29	21	5	33	20	12	11	27	6	25	19	10	16	3	1	22	14	17
(crime rate)		0	0	0	0	0	0	0	0	0	0	0	0	1	1	1	1	2	2	3	4	4	4	5	5	6	8	8	8	12	16	22
1. Garages next to house	4.9	X	X		X			X	X	X		X		X	X	X	X						X	X	X	X	X		X	X	X	X
2. Garage courts or alleyways	4.6					X					X						X	X		X				X	X		X	X		X		X
3. Garages in rear garden, access from alley or court	9.5										X			X	X	X		X							X	X			X			
4. Layouts with few garages	0.4				X				X				X						X								X					X
5. Grid street layouts	6.3												X	X									X			X		X		X		X
6. Cul-de-sac road systems (includes loop roads)	1.9	X	X	X	X	X	X	X	X	X	X	X		X	X			X	X	X		X		X	X	X	X		X	X		
7. Cul-de-sac roads linked to footpath networks	1.9	X	X	X	X	X	X	X	X	X	X	X		X	X			X	X	X		X		X	X		X	X		X	X	

Table 6.4   Thefts from garages in Harrow showing security at different locations

State of security	Garages at the side of house	Garages away from the house
Locked garages	0	7
Unlocked garages	21	5

Source: Poyner, Helson and Webb (1985)

Secondly, although it is not the intention of this report to venture into non-crime issues of design, the evidence about garage theft suggested a more general design policy in providing garage space. The easily observable fact is that in many modern developments home owners frequently do not park their cars in garages because the garage is heavily in use for storage and perhaps some current DIY project. There is a case here to recommend garages to be provided only when they can be supervised from the house. Placing garages at the side of the house, or even further to the rear next to a secure garden area, makes sense of the crime data and the emerging pattern of garage use as storage or workshop accommodation.

Two recommendations emerge:

Garages are best planned next to the house with access from the front of the house facing the street.

Not only are garages safer near to the house, but it enhances their role as providing valuable storage space, typically including a freezer, gardening equipment and furniture, as well as recreational uses such as a DIY workshop.

More dramatic evidence, that the provision of garages separate from the house is often an unsustainable design solution, comes from Northampton. Since fieldwork was done on north-east Northampton during the late 1980s a number of garages in parking courts have been demolished. Where garages had little or no surveillance from nearby houses they were often vandalised, even wrecked, and certainly left unused. All that now remains of these garages is the concrete floor bases for use as open parking bays. Even now these parking bays are largely left unused by residents who see them as risky places to leave their cars. A similar recent observation is that doors to some garages in the back alleyways of Layout Area 1 have clearly been boarded up to avoid break-ins and, presumably, secured for use as storage or workspace rather than as a garage for a vehicle.

Thefts from outside the house

Although thefts from around the outside of the house are officially recorded as a miscellaneous category, there are several small but quite distinct groups of crimes. The classification in Table 6.5 remains almost the same as in the original study of 1982 data.

The map in Figure 6.3 shows the distribution of these thefts across the 38 Layout Areas. It has some similarities to the previous maps for electrical goods burglary and car crime. It is clear that there are layouts that have high and low levels of theft, and several areas are virtually or actually crime-free.

Table 6.5 Theft outside the house in north-east Northampton in 1987

Crime type	Number of crimes	Rate per 1000 households
Bicycles (from gardens and driveways)	56	4.0
Milk, parcels, etc. taken from doorsteps	25	1.8
Clothes from washing lines	25	1.8
Plants and garden ornaments stolen	17	1.2
Property taken from external meter boxes	7	0.5
Other theft outside the house	27	1.9
Total theft outside the house	157	11.2

Source: Based on information from Poyner and Webb (1991)

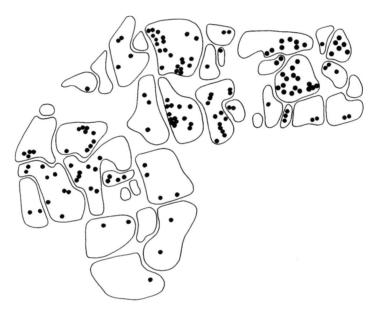

Figure 6.3 Map of thefts from around the home, as listed in Table 6.5

An analysis of this map distribution is shown in Figure 6.4 (at the end of this section). The analysis concentrates on various characteristics of the front and back areas around the house, but first, in the light of the earlier discussion, a direct comparison is included of grid versus cul-de-sac streets in lines 1 and 2. As indicated by the average rates for these two lines, the grid streets show a slight advantage, but it is clear from the rest of the analysis that other aspects are more influential than street pattern.

The question of streets being overlooked by houses (line 3) does have a role in these crimes. This has an average crime rate of 7.3 compared with grid streets of 8.3 and is probably a more important factor.

All the characteristics listed in lines 4–11 appear to be favourable in reducing theft. The more measures there are to protect the back garden the better. This is best illustrated in line 5 for gardens being planned back to back. The good score for a garage opening onto a back alley (line 4) may seem odd, but it probably implies that the construction of a garage at the back reduces access to the rear garden and perhaps provides safer storage in the garage. The small numbers of Layout Areas with this kind of design can only point to the desirability of more detailed studies of this topic should it be possible to fund further work.

Access to the rear garden is also seen as safer if it is gained through a gate at the front of the house (line 6). Other features which give space at the front of the house help to reduce theft. They include the presence of driveways (line 7); garages next to the house, which perhaps provide useful storage (line 9); and front gardens of 3–5 metres (line 11). A more established garden with foliage (trees and shrubs) seems to have a positive influence as does the provision of some front boundary wall, fence or hedge. All the features seem to indicate support for the idea of territoriality where an established and clearly marked front garden area helps to reduce theft from the front of a house and perhaps also to discourage illicit access from the front to the rear. The mechanism works best in a street with potential surveillance from neighbouring houses and possibly other users of the street.

These conclusions are most reinforced by the findings in lines 11 and 12, which make it clear that small front gardens and back gardens with back gates are the main source of insecurity for these types of crime.

These findings are readily understood if we go back to the notes on the early 1982 data study where more detail about the thefts was available to the research team. The following brief notes are based on the first project report (Poyner, Helson and Webb, 1985).

Theft of milk, parcels and other items from doorsteps

Although only 11 cases of stolen milk bottles were examined in fieldwork at Northampton during the first study the report was able to say:

> *These thefts occurred mainly in poorer housing. Most were from pre-1914 terraced houses with front doors opening directly onto the street, often facing the end of or side of other housing and not having the benefit of surveillance from the houses opposite. One New Town Corporation house had a very similar modern equivalent of a front door opening onto a footpath but not overlooked by other houses. Two older council houses in visually exposed positions and with shallow front gardens were also victimised.*

This category of crime has been augmented to include parcels and other items as these emerged in the 1987 data, as did theft from meter boxes included in a cupboard next to the front door on some new housing. These data point to a serious need to consider how these items can be left by delivery services when residents are out or unable to respond when a caller knocks at their door.

There can be no single solution to this but designers should take the issue seriously. There does seem to be a case for some buffer space between the public street and the front door. Whether this really justifies a more traditional front garden or a space such as a portico or porch with a secure cupboard or some similar provision is for designers to decide. The point was made in *Crime Free Housing* that one of the reasons why tenants commonly added porches to the council houses they had purchased was that this provided a safer place to leave deliveries under cover and out of sight.

There is a need for somewhere safe to leave milk and other deliveries out of sight of the street.

Perhaps it is worth considering adding a cautionary note that whatever design is created for this purpose it must not be susceptible to abuse such as enabling someone to hide next to the front door out of sight or able to break-in through a delivery chute or cupboard. It may be that the best route is to develop the function of meter-reading boxes that appear as rather unsightly add-ons to the front or side of new houses. Some thefts were reported from these items of equipment in the Northampton 1987 data, but perhaps a more carefully considered design could integrate the meters and secure space for deliveries into the same cupboard-like unit close to the front door.

No doubt many will argue that this is now out of date in 2002, but perhaps part of the reason for the decline in deliveries of milk and bread is due to this issue of safety alongside the growth of super-market shopping. But, with more and more people living in single-person or all-working families that leave houses unoccupied for substantial periods each day, and with newer forms of distribution such as deliveries from mail order and Internet shopping, surely this issue is important.

Thefts of plants and garden ornaments

This is not a major crime problem, but one which does get reported and one that is likely to be heavily under-recorded. Again this report can do no better than quote from the earlier report (Poyner et al, 1985):

> *Nearly all these are thefts from front gardens of plants, pot-plants or ornamental features such as gates, urns, gnomes and lanterns. They are usually privately owned houses with rather open and exposed front gardens on busy pedestrian routes.*

> *There is some affinity to vandalism in that some of the thefts seem to be more like pranks or skylarking with probably a little drunkenness in some cases, rather than a genuine attempt to remove something of value. The thefts usually occur overnight. It is noticeable that the houses selected as targets tend to be somewhat differentiated from surrounding houses. Particularly up-market houses receive this kind of attention, as well as houses that have extremely well-kept fronts or that have a noticeably large amount of ornaments at the front.*

The issue cannot be regarded as of great importance to housing design but it should be given some consideration. Looking at current trends in housing planning it might be argued that the best solution is to abandon the front garden and so eliminate the risk, but where this approach to planning has been adopted (for example after the Essex Design Guide 1987) residents still use planters, tubs and other ornaments in front of their home creating a similar risk.

The point that seemed to emerge from the early Harrow data was that most of these thefts occurred along well used pedestrian routes from pubs, tube stations and centres of evening life.

It may be that houses along well-used pedestrian routes from evening entertainment and transport services need more protection – at least a buffer area between the house and public sidewalk/street perhaps with waist-high iron railings.

This is not intended as a design recommendation but merely to draw attention to a little recognised crime risk in residential areas.

Having made these points it might be right to place some responsibility for reducing this risk on the householder by using planting and ornamentation that is difficult to steal. Heavy planters are unlikely to be carried off as a prank and well established evergreen and climbing plants will provide foliage with little risk of theft and little damage.

Bicycle theft

Cycle parking is as important (as car parking), but often overlooked. As well as designated parking near to popular destinations thought should be given to where people will leave their bike when they get home. Urban Design Compendium (Llewelyn-Davis, 2000)

The theft of bicycles from around the house is a miniature example of how visibility and accessibility work to provide safe places to leave bicycles. Here, by using comments from the early studies in Harrow and Northampton and by reworking data on theft from around the house published in *Crime Free Housing* we have a simple example of how housing design influences this type of criminal behaviour.

Bicycles are stolen from front gardens, driveways and back gardens (as well as garages, as discussed earlier). In the 1982 data, where we had more detailed information, the victims were most often boys of school age who left their bikes outside their own home or occasionally someone else's home. Thefts tended to happen in the evening or overnight; bicycles were presumably left and not missed until someone remembered about putting it away.

The difference between Harrow and Northampton data was revealing. Table 6.6 shows how the number of bicycle thefts split between front and back gardens in the 1982 samples.

Table 6.6   The location of 49 bicycle thefts from earlier 1982 data (more detail available)

Location of theft	Harrow	Northampton
Back garden	5	11
Front garden or driveway	12	3
Side garden	1	–
Outside house but not known where	8	9
Totals	26	23

Source: Poyner, Helson and Webb (1985)

On the reasonable assumption that 'outside the house' probably means at the front of the house, the table reveals different patterns for Northampton and Harrow. There are comparatively few thefts from back gardens in Harrow but more in Northampton. When we looked at the locations of thefts in the back gardens, they were nearly all insecure back gardens with gates leading from side passageways and back or side footpaths. In Northampton, the design of the New Town public sector housing and the old pre-1914 terraced houses with their footpaths and back lanes offers plenty of opportunity for thieves to get into back gardens even with full height walls or fences. Interestingly, the New Town housing typically has timber gates of slatted construction which make it relatively easy to see through into the garden and also easy to reach through to open a bolt.

In Harrow, where most gardens are back to back or side to side, there were few thefts from back gardens. Because the housing all faces onto the street in Harrow, with relatively open front gardens or drives, any bicycle left at the front is highly vulnerable. Also, the street pattern in Harrow is such that most streets are through-routes and there did seem to be a tendency for these thefts to occur on the streets which are well used as pedestrian routes. (Poyner, Helson and Webb, 1985)

Taking these observations at face value might lead a designer to argue that you can't win – whichever type of house form you adopt people will leave bicycles around and thieves will steal them if still around after dark. But this is the lazy way to view the problem. It is understandable why rear gardens are insecure in the Northampton New Town developments and points to some improvement in rear garden security. The evidence from Harrow seems to confirm that back gardens with no rear access have no thefts from the rear. Further observation of Harrow housing reveals that quite often the gaps between houses are filled by garages or house extensions closing off easy access from the front to rear and perhaps making it difficult for, notably children, to easily park their bicycles out of sight at the back of the house. These design characteristics of much of the Harrow housing also suggest that the tendency to leave garages open or unlocked may be connected to this problem – a problem already mentioned under 'Theft from garages'.

Clearly, the matter is open to creative thinking by designers, but one (conventional) solution is to create access from the front to a secure garden (or yard) at the back of a house. The rear garden can be secure as long as there is a gated access that can be locked when not in use, and that can be supervised from inside the house while children or others come and go. This arrangement is typical of traditional suburban houses of the 1930s.

The 1987 data from *Crime Free Housing* helps to confirm that this approach to security of the back garden is effective. Figure 6.4 shows that thefts from outside the house are lowest in the layouts where gardens are back to back (line 5) and where there is a front gate access to the rear garden (line 6). The importance of avoiding access to the back garden from the back is indicated in line 12 of Figure 6.4.

> *The problem of bicycle theft supports the idea of ensuring a secure back yard or garden to every house, with a gated access from the street (front of the house).*

An alternative to this arrangement might be to provide the gated access off a driveway at the side of the house, but it would be more difficult to cover this access by surveillance when the house was unoccupied. The advantage of a gate on the front face of the house facing the street is that it benefits from surveillance from the street and neighbouring houses.

A current planning trend is to abandon front gardens in housing design in pursuit of higher densities and creating attractive urban spaces – see, for example, the Essex Design Guide (Essex Planning Officers Association, 1997: 28ff.). It is difficult to work out from historical evidence what effect this might have on thefts from the front of the house. The implication from the data in Figure 6.4 is that moderate-sized gardens (line 11) are better than small front gardens (line 13) which have a particularly problematic reputation. Other guidance talks of a 1.5m to 3m semi-private strip between residential buildings and the public pavement to provide space for a small garden, bicycle stand, seating and for services such as rubbish collection and meter-reading (Lewelyn-Davis, 2000). Clearly, these issues are not well resolved in current housing design, but at least the design requirements are being clarified.

Clothes stolen from washing lines

This set of crimes will seem trivial to most readers and is certainly small, but it was surprising to the research team during the early research to find such a clear crime set emerge.

All thefts were from back gardens.

No offenders were caught but two were seen taking items from washing lines, both were men taking items of women's underwear. One ran off when the victim saw him and banged on the window; the other was seen climbing over the back fence. However, in only 8 of the total 24 cases we had in the study were the items taken limited to women's underwear. Other clothing and some towels and sheets were taken. So, the motive probably varies from a degree of sexual interest to 'straight' theft.

On visiting locations of thefts in Northampton, we found that most of the washing lines could easily be seen from well used paths or alleyways. It seemed likely that the items stolen had caught the eye of the offender as he passed, even at night. In most cases access was from the rear footpaths, service roads or the alleyways of older housing.

What makes it interesting in the context of this report is that the levels of such theft in Harrow were so much lower than those in the 1982 Northampton data (see Table 6.7). Again, as with bicycles it has much to do with the fact that in Harrow most gardens are back to back and so washing hung in back gardens is not visible to anyone walking past in the street.

Table 6.7   Comparison of theft of clothes from washing lines

| | Harrow | Northampton | |
	1982	1982	1987
Number of thefts in sample	5	19	25
Rate of thefts per 1000 households	0.3	3.3	1.8
Sources: Poyner , Helson and Webb (1985) and Poyner and Webb (1991)			

The lesson from this crime set has much in common with bicycle theft in that:

A back garden or yard is most secure if it is out of sight of pedestrian routes and only accessible via well secured and supervised gated access. It also implies well maintained and full-height walls or fences (circa 1.8m).

It should perhaps be noted that line 4 of Figure 6.4 suggests that gardens with garages opening onto back alleyways or garage courts have low levels of garden theft. The obvious problem with this result is that it is based on only four examples. But it might be that this arrangement can be made more secure by providing good surveillance of the back of houses and when much more substantial construction is used than a lightweight timber fence with a gate of similar construction. Research cannot always give definitive answers, but this is a design issue open to more thought and experiment. Note also that garages in this situation will need more security treatment than if accessed from the front of the house.

Figure 6.4 Analysis of design and layout factors for theft from outside the home

LAYOUT AREAS →	13	16	12	1	15	31	33	34	10	3	11	24	2	14	19	22	6	17	27	5	28	36	25	38	7	32	21	26	35	20	29	CRIME RATES IN RANK ORDER →
	0	0	2	3	3	5	5	6	6	7	7	7	8	8	8	8	10	10	11	11		12	16	16	17	17	18	19	20	23	24	10.1
1. Grid street layouts			X			X							X				X				X		X	X		X	X	X	X	X	X	8.3
2. Cul-de-sac road systems										X			X	X	X	X	X				X	X	X	X		X	X	X	X	X	X	10.7
3. Streets overlooked by houses along both sides	X	X	X	X	X	X	X	X	X	X	X	X	X	X	X	X	X	X	X	X	X	X	X	X		X	X	X	X	X	X	7.3
4. Garages in rear garden, access by alley or court	X	X								X			X	X			X															5.7
5. Gardens mostly back onto other gardens	X	X	X	X						X			X	X			X	X														6.4
6. Front gate to back garden	X	X	X	X								X	X	X		X	X	X	X		X		X	X								6.9
7. Houses with private driveways	X	X	X		X	X	X						X	X	X	X	X	X	X		X		X	X	X							7.6
8. Front garden boundaries – fence/walls/hedge	X	X	X			X	X	X	X	X		X	X	X	X	X	X	X	X									X				7.6
9. Garages next to the house	X	X	X						X	X			X	X	X	X	X	X		X			X			X						8.0
10. Foliage in front of the house	X						X	X	X	X		X	X	X	X	X	X		X	X			X	X								8.1
11. Front gardens 3–5 metres	X		X					X	X	X		X	X	X	X	X	X	X	X	X	X		X	X				X				8.2
12. Back gate to garden							X	X		X										X	X		X					X	X	X	X	12.7
13. Small front gardens			X															X		X			X					X	X	X	X	16.4
14. Terraced houses			X	X	X			X	X	X			X							X			X	X		X	X	X	X	X	X	12.7

Thefts of motorcycles

Recorded under motor vehicle theft, these are thefts of mopeds, scooters and motorcycles. In the first study the two research locations had different patterns. In Harrow thefts were mainly of motorcycles but in Northampton most were mopeds. The general impression was that the bikes are stolen in a relatively unplanned manner, having been seen left in the street or in the front garden of a terraced house. Most were recovered intact.

The data from the 1982 studies was presented in the original report as in Table 6.8.

This preliminary data points to the risk being from street parking and in the front driveways in Harrow and communal parking bays of Northampton New Town housing. Even when bikes were taken from 'safer' places such as a garage or back garden, the detail supports the general case.

The two thefts from garages appear to be from poorly supervised garages in little use. Neither theft was discovered for some days. The single case of theft from the back garden was of a motorcycle left there for the owner to do some repair work; again the theft was not reported for some days, implying that there was little supervision and certainly little security.

Table 6.8 Locations from which motorcycles were stolen (1982 data)

Location	Harrow	Northampton
Garage	0	2
Back garden	0	1
Driveway/front garden	5	1
Parking areas/bays	0	4
Street outside house	7	5
Location not known	4	4
	16	17

Source: Poyner, Helson and Webb (1985)

These observations led to a similar conclusion as with bicycles: owners of motorcycles do not appear to have the opportunity to store vehicles in a more suitable space. If we look at the mapped distribution of motorcycle theft in the 1987 Northampton data (Figure 6.5) and the matrix analysis Figure 6.6 at the end of this section it is clear (in the matrix line 1) that this theft is strongly correlated to lower-income housing.

Here is an interesting example of data that points to strong socio-economic explanations of the map distribution that would be associated with a more conventional criminological perspective. Here is clear evidence that it could be local offenders living in the poorer housing that steal the motorbikes and it also suggests that the residents of poorer areas are more likely to own and use motorbikes, particularly mopeds and scooters.

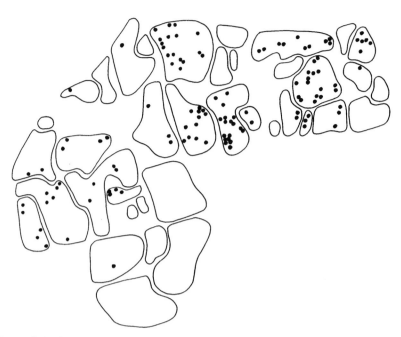

Figure 6.5 Map of theft of motorcycles from north-east Northampton (1987 data)

Although we can acknowledge that these socio-economic and criminological factors might largely explain the map distribution, an alternative design explanation is also relevant. The matrix in Figure 6.6 sets out some of the elements of housing design that might help or hinder the provision of safe storage for motorcycles around the house. The visual pattern is clear enough to see the difference between lines 2–5 and 6–9 in the matrix. The average crime rates for each line strongly reinforce this pattern.

On the face of it, it can be argued strongly from this evidence that in housing with attached garages (2) and private drives (4) with 3–5 metre front gardens (5) and a gated access at the front of the house to a garden at the rear (3), there is practically no motorcycle theft. (Note that the first 10 columns represent Layout Areas with zero crime rates.) However, with no private driveways (6), or small front gardens (9), access to rear gardens only through a back gate (7) and shared parking areas (8), then motorcycles will be stolen. It can also be seen from the matrix that the best places for leaving motorcycles are garages next to the house or a secure back garden with access from the front (lines 2 and 3).

These findings make a strong case for designing easier access for motorcycles to be wheeled into a secure back garden/yard or access to garaging or sheds close to the house.

Figure 6.6 Analysis of design and layout factors for theft of motorcycles

LAYOUT AREAS																															
CRIME RATES IN RANK ORDER → →	38	34	28	24	22	16	14	13	12	10	17	15	3	11	36	6	5	2	31	33	19	1	27	21	32	26	20	35	7	29	25
av. 7.5	0	0	0	0	0	0	0	0	0	0	2	3	3	3	4	4	5	6	6	7	8	13	13	15	18	19	20	21	22	23	25
1. Lower-income households — 12.6													X				X		X			X	X	X	X	X	X	X	X	X	X
2. Garage next to house — 2.5	X	X	X	X	X	X	X	X	X	X	X	X	X	X	X								X								
3. Front gate to back garden — 2.7	X	X	X	X	X	X	X	X	X	X	X	X	X		X	X	X							X							
4. Houses with private driveways — 2.9	X	X	X	X	X	X	X	X	X	X	X	X	X		X	X	X	X	X	X				X							
5. Front gardens 3–5 metres — 4.2	X	X	X	X	X	X	X	X	X	X	X	X	X		X	X	X	X	X	X				X							
5. On-street parking (in front of houses) — 6.9									X				X			X	X	X				X									
6. Houses do not have private driveways — 13.9											X	X	X			X	X						X	X	X	X	X	X	X	X	X
7. Back gate to garden — 14.1											X	X	X			X	X	X					X	X	X	X	X	X	X	X	X
8. Shared off-street parking — 16.8											X						X					X	X	X	X	X	X	X	X	X	X
9. Small front gardens — 17.9															X	X	X						X	X	X	X	X	X	X	X	X
10. Grid street layouts — 7.1										X	X	X	X				X					X				X		X		X	
11. Cul-de-sac road systems — 8.1											X	X	X	X		X	X	X	X	X			X	X	X	X	X	X	X	X	X

Criminal damage

Criminal damage or vandalism has always been seen as a major problem in housing, particularly in the public-sector housing estates with mainly medium- and high-rise apartment blocks. Indeed, the publication in Britain of Newman's book *Defensible Space* was seen to be most relevant by British architects to the problems of vandalism and, for example, coincided with the publication, also by the Architectural Press, of Colin Ward's equally stimulating book *Vandalism* (Newman, 1973; Ward, 1973; Poyner, 1983: chapter 5).

However, the issue of vandalism has been much less serious in low-rise housing, except for some of the worst managed British council estates. In the first study with 1982 data, a classification was developed with the following analysis in Table 6.9.

As can be seen from the table, the dominant feature of the crime record in Harrow was of criminal damage to the property of Asian households. This can be attributed to the fact that a significant proportion of households were of Asian background at the time[1]. No such issue emerged in the Northampton data. By the time 1987 data was collected it was not possible to obtain the same level of detail, so a simpler classification was used, as already shown in Table 6.2. The inclusion of racial victimisation was more controversial in the 1980s than now. It is only since 1999 that national crime statistics record 'Racially-aggravated criminal damage to a dwelling'. This category is small but growing. If the Harrow and Northampton studies had been carried out in today's climate a more data-rich study would now be possible.

With the less detailed 1987 data, a map was drawn up of criminal damage incidents that involved broken glass in windows and doors of houses caused by thrown stones or air gun pellets, as well as other damage. It seemed likely that much of this behaviour was the result of rowdy and malicious behaviour by youths and children and some may well involve victimisation of a number of unfortunate individuals, but the data was not available to make judgements. However, like the other maps, the distribution had a distinctive pattern showing that mainly the public sector housing was suffering this damage (Figure 6.7).

Table 6.9   Criminal damage to residential property in Harrow and Northampton 1982

Crime rates per 1000 households	Harrow N	Harrow N/1000	N'pton N	N'pton N/1000
Rowdy youths	22	1.3	3	0.5
Victimisation of:				
Asian households	37	2.2	0	0.0
Other households	17	1.0	8	1.4
Air gun attacks	6	0.4	0	0.0
Arson	2	0.1	5	0.9
Other	5	0.3	2	0.3
Totals	89	5.3	18	3.1

Source: Poyner, Helson and Webb (1985)

1. According to the 1981 census the population in the Harrow study area with the head of household being born in the New Commonwealth or Pakistan averaged 16.14%, rising to 27% in one of the wards. By comparison the proportion for Northampton was only 4.82%.

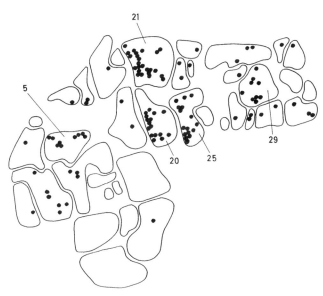

Figure 6.7   Map distribution of criminal damage (broken glass in doors and windows)

Broadly, two hypotheses emerged. One about physical design observed that most of the areas with damage were areas with green open space:

> *Even within the public sector there is a clear concentration in areas 20, 21 and 25, with 29 and 5 showing less of a problem. All these areas are large public housing estates and unlike other housing areas the houses face onto communal greens with footpaths often running close to the front of the houses. At the same time the small front gardens are usually open grass areas. It is easy to imagine that such design forms do promote the more rowdy activities of youths and children which lead to damage of the type described. If this design form does create the increased risk, then the remedy would be to avoid designs with communal open space in front of housing. Although the thinness of our data would lead us to be cautious about making a strong recommendation, it has to be admitted that housing layouts with conventional streets had little trouble. (Poyner and Webb, 1991: 82)*

The message from this seems to be that there is evidence enough to suggest that more detailed study of criminal damage in residential areas would produce useful guidance, but for the purposes of this report the evidence is as yet not strong enough. However, as an interim suggestion the following might provide a useful guide:

> **The planning of communal green spaces should be carefully considered in relation to the frontages of housing. Where it is likely to be used by children and youths, some separation should be provided through protective landscaping and/or the presence of a well used carriageway.**

It also acts as a reminder that the whole issue of designing residential areas that can absorb or cater for activities of young people has not emerged from studies of residential crime. It is also fair to comment that a search through the recommendations of many of the planning and design guides in current use by planning and urban design professionals reveals a failure to address the issue. To this end it is worth noting the work by two architectural liaison officers on a good practice guide on the provision and design of youth shelters as places where young people can gather safely and without causing nuisance to local residents (Hampshire and Wilkinson, 1999).

The concept for this update project was to review already available research rather than to obtain new data. Recognising the limitations of this approach it was proposed and accepted that at least some fresh data might be obtained for one or two case studies aimed at illustrating and confirming the findings from *Crime Free Housing*. During the course of the project contact was made with planners and police officers from Northampton. It was a pleasant surprise to discover that recent initiatives, under the Crime and Disorder Act, were being carried out in the north-eastern part of the area used for the layout studies. These initiatives were being carried out under the acronym of CASPAR (Crime and Anti-Social behaviour PARtnership).

A pilot project had been carried out on the Bellinge estate, which was just south of the *Crime Free Housing* study area and had become one the most crime-ridden areas of Northampton. The seriousness of the problems that led to this pilot was summed up in the following quotation from a project report:

> *Although some community safety works had been carried out in the early 1990s these have not proved to be successful and things came to a head in 1996 when a police raid, aimed at stopping the sale of drugs, was carried out. This raid resulted in large-scale public disorder and the closing of the public house but the drug dealing operation simply moved into other areas of the estate. (Methven, 2001)*

A mixed programme of social and physical change then followed and was quite successful in reducing crime. Of particular interest to this report was the work done on the estate to block off many of the rabbit warren of footways that permeated the 1970s development and was thought to make the area impossible to police and an ideal environment for criminals to find good cover and easy means of escape.

On the basis of this success the CASPAR projects were developed. The first (CASPAR 1) was centred on the Blackthorn estate, identified in the *Crime Free Housing* study as Layout Area 29. The first point of interest to this study was to discover that Layout Area 29 had become a 'hot spot' of crime in the minds of the police and the local authority. In the 1987 data, it was the worst area for theft around the home and second worst area for car theft and motorcycle theft but for other crimes it was not the worst by any means.

The next point of interest was that the measures actually taken to improve the Blackthorn estate were substantially physical in nature:

> *Year one of the CASPAR 1 project in Blackthorn was allocated £200,000 from the Housing Capital budget and this is being used to update lighting, clear sight lines by the removal of trees and shrubs, install motorcycle barriers and barriers against joy riders in cars and extend gardens to avoid dead spaces where people can conceal themselves easily. Much of the work on landscaping is being carried out around the middle and lower schools in order to ensure that children travelling to and from these locations can do so safely. (Methven, 2001)*

It seems clear that the first major efforts were about cleaning up the area. Many skips of rubbish were collected, much of it with self-help residents action. A much speeded up abandoned car policy was introduced to remove cars more quickly and contracts were organised to cut back and clear excessive overgrown trees and shrubs. It is interesting to see that these problems have developed over the years because the design of the area creates a considerable demand for this kind of maintenance. Litter can easily be spread through the semi-private areas of these estates, and abandoned vehicle are easily left in communal parking bays for which no resident has any proprietary control. Abandoned vehicles are not generally left in streets where there is only parking on private drives. The need for cutting back trees and shrubs is again a product of the landscape planting all over these estates, and it is the responsibility of the housing authority to maintain it.

Other initiatives were considered including work with known offenders and the police began with targeting known individuals. There were three evictions and an arrest of a repeat offender early in 2000. The programme of physical improvements to footpaths and underpasses etc. was planned to be carried on in the following years and has received further funding. At the time this project was examined it was only possible to obtain information about the first year. It has continued through 2001. According to press information (see cutting below) the overall level of crime has fallen from a peak in 1998 of 832 crimes to only 292 in 2001.

Crime prevention win

The Office of the Deputy Prime Minister's Urban Renaissance Award was won by a crime prevention scheme on the Blackthorn Estate in Northampton. The scheme reduced crime rates on the estate from 832 reported crimes in 1998 to 292 reported crimes a year in 2001. The project was led by Northampton Borough Council, the police and Northamptonshire County Council.

Cutting from *Building Design* for 8 November 2002

This situation seemed to be well worth further investigation to see what connection could be found between the original 1987 data on this area and how the patterns of crime might have changed, bearing in mind that at least part of the original study areas had become identified as a major problem and had received what was believed to be a successful crime prevention initiative. A request was made, and agreed to, to provide crime data for the eastern end of the original study area which included Areas 27 to 38 (see Figure 7.1).

The title of 'Fifteen years on' is not so much intended to refer to the crime data, which to be strictly accurate is only 13 years on from 1987. What was really referred to was that fieldwork observations of these Layout Areas 27–38 were made roughly 15 years apart. During the original research ordnance survey maps were not available for the newest developments on the extreme eastern edge (Areas 34–38). Area 37 had been further developed to almost exactly twice its size (from 84 to 170 houses) and a number of other changes could be seen with a discerning eye.

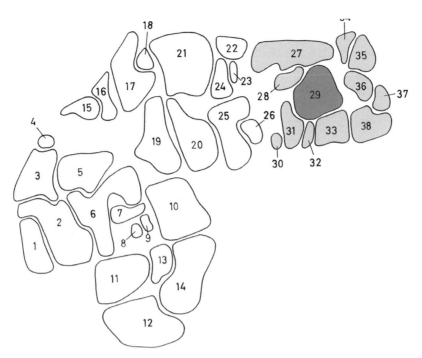

Figure 7.1   Part of the study area for which 2000 data was assembled

As this was not designed to be an in-depth analysis, it was decided to accept information on crime under the officially recorded categories rather than attempt to reconstruct the crime classification of the original study. There would be some distortion in the data, for example 2000 figures for thefts of vehicles would include motorcycles, and thefts from vehicles would include thefts of external components. The principal anomaly in the burglary data would be the inclusion of attempts in 2000, the 1987 data being simply the addition of the two major crime sets of electrical goods and cash and jewellery burglary. Nevertheless, even bearing these anomalies in mind, they should not undermine the general conclusions drawn from the following analyses which focus on changes in distribution of these crimes rather than overall changes in incidence.

Burglary

Figure 7.2 compares the two maps of burglary for 1987 and 2000. Interestingly both maps have very similar numbers of crimes (95 and 97 respectively) but it is quite clear that the distribution has shifted. Some areas have more crime and others less. It is possible to argue that there is a drop in crime since 1987 because the 2000 data includes attempted burglary. But we already know that there will be some reduction in burglary from the CASPAR 1 project. What is much more interesting is the direction of change that has occurred in each of the 10 layout areas large enough to be analysed in the main study (over 100 houses). This is diagrammed in Figure 7.3.

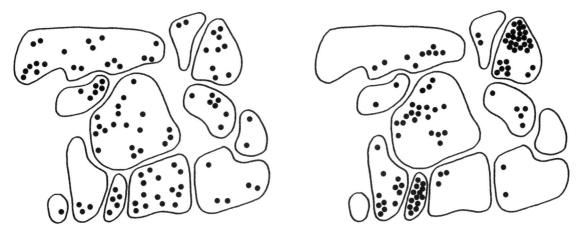

Figure 7.2 Maps for burglary for 1987 and 2000 data

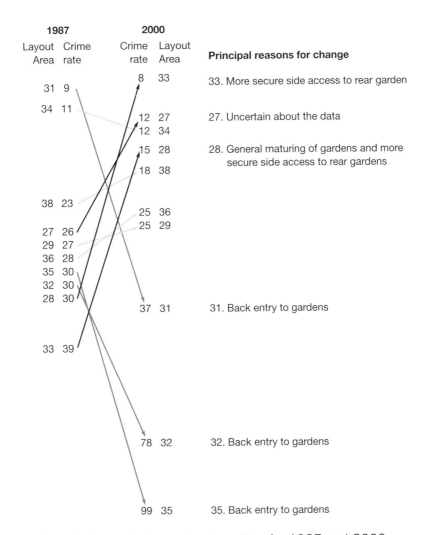

Figure 7.3 Direction of change between burglary data for 1987 and 2000

In Figure 7.3 the two sets of crime rates are listed side by side for each of the 10 layout areas with over 100 houses. There is certainly no general pattern of rise or fall so often assumed by statisticians preoccupied by attempts to monitor trends. Here there is something much more dynamic occurring over time. Perhaps we should briefly consider Area 29 at the centre of the maps in Figures 7.1 and 7.2 (and midway down the list in Figure 7.3). These data were taken from a period when the CASPAR 1 project was well underway. It appears that either the project has had little effect on burglary or the burglary level in Area 29 has been much higher. It seems quite likely that it was higher from comments by police, although one change which seems to have been made to the burglary pattern was that after much of the obscuring foliage from trees and shrubs in Area 29 was cut back there had been a tendency for burglary to switch from daytime to evening rather than be prevented.

Ignoring the light grey arrows in Figure 7.3 the diagram clearly shows that three layout areas have reduced in burglary while three have dramatically increased. Can a reliable rational reason be found for this? Reviewing the changes that have taken place in this part of Northampton it is hard to attribute this change to the CASPAR 1 initiatives. For example, of the three areas that increased in crime two (31 and 32) were included in lighting improvements but 35 was not. However, all three of these areas have similar design characteristics. From the burglary point of view they are terraced houses not on through-streets, the back gardens are all accessible from rear paths or parking bays and in turn these are connected to the segregated pedestrian network of paths. These are all factors identified as a problem for burglary and it can be said that these layouts are 'bad designs'.

In *Crime Free Housing* Area 31 was discussed as an example of public-sector housing that had little crime except for thefts from cars. It attempted to explain why the back paths for this terraced housing did not create a problem for burglary:

> . . . *the pathways passing along the backs of the housing in Area 31 have been designed as much more private areas which are controlled and supervised by house occupants. The housing is separated into small groups of houses which are arranged back-to-back to form a protective 'courtyard' type of area in the centre through which the pathways pass. Access into these back paths is only through narrow alleyways which are not easily noticed on first driving into the area...Children's play spaces are provided in these central areas, and the effect of all this is that they become an extension of the rear garden. There is good supervision from the surrounding houses, as gardens only have small waist-high fences, and parents can and do easily control their children in the play spaces. In effect, the houses in Area 31 have been designed 'inside out' so that the rear gardens become the front gardens which face onto a well-supervised pedestrian cul-de-sac. (Poyner and Webb, 1991: 88–9)*

Honesty being the best policy makes it necessary to admit that this was a rather forced attempt to explain the low burglary levels. It might have worked initially, but the 2000 data suggests that in the long run it is not easy to resist the general principle that easy access to back gardens is likely to lead to burglary. This example supports the notion that high-crime areas can take time to develop – as their weaknesses are learned by local burglars and increasingly exploited. The process will be helped by the development of mature gardens with much more cover from growing hedges, shrubs and trees.

Of the three arrows indicating a fall in burglary, Area 27 (top left area in maps in Figure 7.2) may have misleading data. The top half of this area had no crime reported in 2000 even though it was one of the high crime areas in 1987. It is almost certain that some data is missing due perhaps to some misunderstanding about the boundary definitions used in requesting data. This seems quite likely because it is believed that the same coding was used to obtain data for this study and the monitoring exercise used to evaluate the CASPAR 1 project area.

So, ignoring the (apparent) improvement to Area 27, why would Areas 33 and 28 improve? The easiest answer is found in Area 33. In the book *Crime Free Housing* there is a brief analysis of the problems giving rise to a high burglary rate for this area.

> . . . *It was discovered that it is comparatively easy to get to the back of many of the houses in this area. The houses have driveways, and therefore there is little theft of cars, but the builder only left spaces for garages to be built, and in many houses the owners have not yet constructed their own garage, leaving the side access to the back garden wide open (see photo). (Poyner and Webb, 1991: 90–1).*

Source: Poyner and Webb (1991: 91)

When the area was revisited fifteen years on, it was easy to see that with maturity most of these houses have blocked off this side access to the back garden, either by constructing a garage or by fencing. In many cases garages had been constructed and set back into the garden with large gates installed to shut off the driveway at the side of the house. In this way the home owners have avoided the need for a side gate between garage and house. No doubt the reason for this arrangement is that the driveways were not wide enough to construct a good sized garage at the side of the house. The photo below of Area 33 was taken during the summer of 2000.

Photo by author

The reason behind the reduction in burglary in Area 28 is less obvious. It may be much the same as that for Area 33 but to be honest no detailed record is available to confirm this. Nevertheless, this area has every sign today of being well kept by most residents and with evidence of improvement to front boundaries of garden it seems quite likely that the access to back gardens has been made more secure over the past 15 years. The photograph below illustrates an obvious example of improvement to the security of a house at the end of one of the cul-de-sacs. The photograph also reveals one of the problems of this Layout Area; there are several footpaths creating plenty of through movement by school children, youths and those with motorbikes.

Photo by author

What seems interesting about these two areas is that unlike the 'bad layouts' with accessible back gardens, these two areas seem to have the basic ingredients for creating a secure back garden and good surveillance at the front due to houses facing across the street. They do not have all the recommended principles but enough to become a low-risk area for burglary. This pattern of change suggests the idea that 'good' gets better but 'bad' designs only get worse. This pattern of change seems to stand out much more clearly than the result of the local crime prevention initiatives in CASPAR 1.

Before going on to look at car crime, another general pattern is worth noting in the burglary data. We know from the analysis in *Crime Free Housing* that the network of footpaths in this end of the study area has an influence on crime. While the distribution of dots in the 1987 data map in Figure 7.2 is relatively evenly spread this is not so with 2000 data. Closer analysis of the footpath system, particularly the routes taken by school children to and from school and by youths walking from the town centre or the nearby shopping centre at Western Favell or related public transport, reveals a clear coincidence with burglary. The principal routes are east–west and shown in Figure 7.4. These lines do not represent all the main paths but they seem to represent the principal lines of movement that have evolved.

The suggested hypothesis is that these routes have evolved over time. As these patterns of movement harden up so crime has become more focused leaving large areas free of burglary risk (represented by the lightly shaded areas). An example might be seen in Area 27 (top left of the map) where there is a distinct line of dots on all three crime maps in Figures 7.2 and 7.4. This is an internal cul-de-sac street obviously used as part of a through pedestrian route. However, the original design for Area 27 has a spine footpath route parallel with this street about 60 metres further north that is relatively little used. Similarly, footpath routes through pedestrian underpasses that were clearly intended for major pedestrian movement have become virtually abandoned in favour of more direct surface routes.

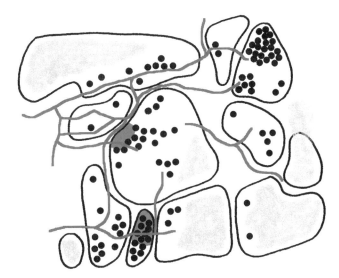

Figure 7.4   Map of 2000 burglary showing principal pedestrian movement

One further point emerged from a questionnaire survey of residents. In general comments written into the questionnaire a resident indicated that drugs were readily available for sale in the areas darkly shaded on the map in Figure 7.4 (McDonnell, 2000). These may not be the only point of sale for illegal drugs but it is clear that there is a relationship between principal pedestrian movement and burglary hot spots.

Car theft

The comparison of theft of cars is problematic because of classification anomalies. Whereas the 1987 data excluded motorcycle theft from our category 'Theft of cars', we must assume that the police data for 2000 includes motorcycle theft. However, despite these important problems with data the comparison is interesting. Figures 7.5 and 7.6 present this comparison.

The first obvious point is that there is much less theft of motor vehicles in 2000. The two maps show 97 crimes in 1987 and only 46 in 2000. If we added in the motorcycle crimes the total would be 138 crimes in the 1987 map. There seems only one general explanation for this, and it must be the general improvement in car security that has occurred nationally. However, if we look at the national statistics more carefully the figures for this normally well-recorded crime are much closer for the two years concerned. The 1987 figure for theft of motor vehicles is 398,600 (Home Office, 1988) and 328,037 for the year 2000/1 (Simmonds et al, 2002). This is a drop of 18% (to 82% of the 1987 figure) whereas the drop in these local figures was to half or a third depending on the figures you choose.

This general improvement in car security probably explains most of the reductions in most areas compared in Figure 7.5, but it seems that the most specific change is the drop in crime for Area 29 in which the CASPAR 1 project was mainly active. A major aspect of this project was the clearing away of excess foliage from overgrown landscaping. Much of this overgrown landscaping was around parking bays and other roadways used for parking. Police officers believe that this has had a major effect on crime as parked cars are now much less hidden or screened by planting and so illegal activity in parking areas has been discouraged.

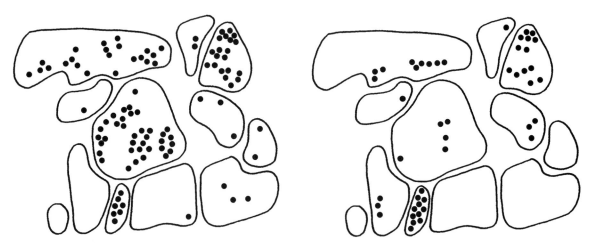

Figure 7.5 Comparison of theft of cars/MV in 1987 and 2000

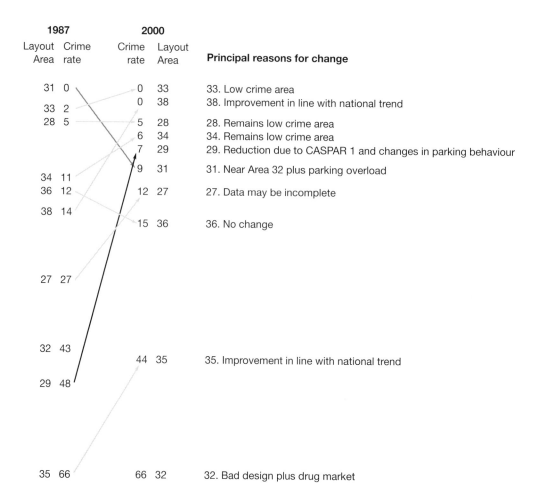

Figure 7.6 Direction of change between theft of cars data for 1987 and 2000

Another point emerged in looking around Area 29 during 2001 and making a special effort to look at parking after six o'clock in the evening and at weekends, when most cars are parked on the estate. Just as Area 33 has adapted to the problem of burglary risk by adding garages and gates over the last 15 years, so adaptations have taken place in parking behaviour. It is quite noticeable that residents in Area 29 avoid parking in the parking bays that are at the back of terraces and otherwise unsupervised. Instead, often quite bizarre parking behaviour has emerged where people park as close to their home as possible often in more exposed and visible positions. The photograph below from the eastern end of Area 29 illustrates this clearly.

Local pattern of parking behaviour that has developed over time in Area 29:

Photo by author

Another parking behaviour preferred to parking in the bays provided is to park along the approach roads into the estate which run along wide grass verges. The pattern is now so well established that it may be preferred because cars are better protected in this location. As can be seen in the next photograph, cars parked in this setting are well clear of passing pedestrian movement and are easily visible to anyone passing through the area. It is also true that by parking nose to tail rather than side by side in parking bays, there is less risk of minor damage to the sides of the car.

Photo by author

The net effect of these adaptive parking behaviours may be to reduce the risk of theft compared with the practice of parking in the bays provided.

More generally, the comments in Figure 7.6 sum up the most likely explanations for the changes in car theft. It picks out only two areas for negative comment. Area 32 emerges as the worst area. It has all the problems of parking bays behind houses and, as has been mentioned in the previous section, is an area with illegal drug sales. Area 31 may be partly influenced by the above as it is a neighbouring development. However, recent observations of this cul-de-sac development reveal a huge parking overload and consequent chaotic parking conditions. In *Crime Free Housing* there is a photograph of this area showing parking on front drives; the more recent photograph (below) illustrates the continuing growth of parking demands in housing.

Photograph of Layout Area 31 after 6.00 pm with most people home from work

Theft from inside cars

Figures 7.7 and 7.8 compare thefts from inside cars in 1987 with recorded incidents of thefts from vehicles in 2000. Overall, the two data sets show roughly the same level of crime (108 in 1987 and 95 in 2000). Comparison, however, is again problematic because the 2000 data will include thefts of external components, a problem excluded from the more precise data set of thefts from inside cars in 1987. Thefts from motorcycles will also be included in the 2000 dataset, although this will be too small to affect the overall pattern greatly. Bearing these anomalies in mind, this would suggest that thefts from vehicles have reduced over this 15-year interval, as we saw in relation to thefts of cars, and is probably again largely due to improved vehicle security.

Despite these anomalies in the two datasets, however, some interesting changes in the distribution of these thefts can be observed from Figures 7.7 and 7.8. Area 29 shows an obvious decrease in crime, associated again with the CASPAR 1 project, while areas 28, 34, 36, 38 and particularly 32 all show increases in these thefts, even taking into account the fact that the 2000 map will include thefts of external components.

How far the concentration of crime in Area 32 is related to the drug problem is not known, but it certainly has problematic parking provision which has become worse over the years, as we discussed earlier. Areas 28, 34, 36 and 38, however, have private drives and garages and were relatively safe areas in 1987. The increases in crime in these areas may be due to the fact that they are all cul-de-sac developments but with footpath routes running through them. Furthermore, these are developments that are now maturing and have much more foliage and so on in the front gardens and more cars parked in the street, changes that will reduce the level of surveillance of the street from the house.

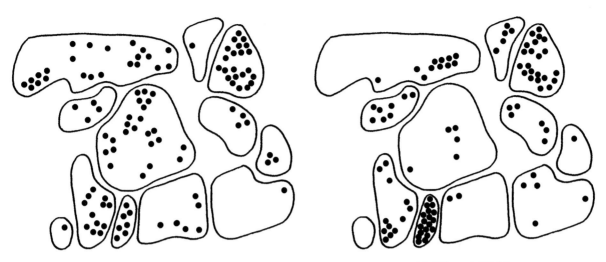

Figure 7.7   Comparison of the distribution of thefts from cars in 1987 and 2000

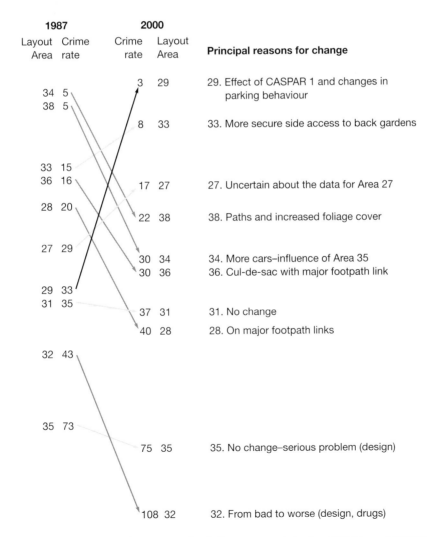

1987		2000		
Layout Area	Crime rate	Crime rate	Layout Area	**Principal reasons for change**
		3	29	29. Effect of CASPAR 1 and changes in parking behaviour
34	5			
38	5			
		8	33	33. More secure side access to back gardens
33	15			
36	16	17	27	27. Uncertain about the data for Area 27
28	20	22	38	38. Paths and increased foliage cover
27	29			
		30	34	34. More cars–influence of Area 35
		30	36	36. Cul-de-sac with major footpath link
29	33			
31	35	37	31	31. No change
		40	28	28. On major footpath links
32	43			
35	73	75	35	35. No change–serious problem (design)
		108	32	32. From bad to worse (design, drugs)

Figure 7.8   Direction of change between theft from cars data for 1987 and 2000

There are two explanations for how these increases in crime have developed. First, it may simply be a case of these footpath routes making areas more accessible with time as they become favourite routes for youths moving about, as we discussed earlier. Secondly, they might be interpreted as a displacement effect from the CASPAR 1 project. The displacement mechanism is more likely to apply to these thefts because they seem to be committed by youths in search of relatively easy targets, and would be facilitated here by the presence of the footpath systems. Wandering the streets eyeing up cars is just about the simplest *modus operandi* available in suburban housing.

Conclusions

The first finding is that while there has been a reduction in car theft and probably theft from cars, burglary has remained at much the same level in both 1987 and 2000. It is assumed that one of the principal reasons for a drop in car crime is due to the national trend in car security.

The impact of the CASPAR 1 project under the Northampton Community Safety Partnership has been very powerful in relation to the two categories of car theft, but it appears to have had little effect on burglary. The reason for the strong effect seems largely due to the removal of landscaping material in the form of overgrown shrubs and trees, particularly around communal parking areas. Increased police activity in the area will have added to this effect, as may have the altered parking behaviour of residents to avoid using the communal parking bays.

Where the Layout Areas have increased their crime level (burglary and theft *from* cars) it can be said that these are areas with significant design faults that appear to only become worse with time. The principal design fault that encourages burglary is easy entry from back paths to back gardens. For thefts *from* cars the principal weaknesses of design are the many footpath connections and general maturity of foliage in front gardens that may reduce surveillance of the street from the houses.

In both crimes there is an emergent principle that if the layout and design is essentially secure to start with, then it will remain safe or improve. This may include designs with the opportunity for improvements to be made by residents. If the design and layout is basically flawed with weaknesses such as insecure back gardens easily entered from back paths, communal parking and extensive networks of footpaths then the problems of crime will often continue to grow. The secondary development of social problems such as the establishment of illegal drug markets seems to emerge in already established crime hot spots. No doubt the selling of drugs and the high crime levels feed off each other.

A note on lighting and fear of crime

Fear of crime and lighting are now seen as important issues in the improvement of high crime estates (particularly those in the public sector). Although the issue was recognised in the early 1980s when the early layout studies were underway, the research objectives were focused on the question of how physical planning was related to crime. For this reason lighting was not seen as of primary concern; it was assumed that for new developments the contemporary standards generated by the lighting industry would be sufficient.

The CASPAR project on the Blackthorn estate provides the opportunity to consider fear and lighting. It is clear from the findings of the project's questionnaire survey that lighting was considered as a serious problem by residents, second only to problems of damage and rubbish – litter and abandoned cars.

Respondents were encouraged to write down places on the estate that they try to avoid. The area near to a few local shops and pub received the highest comments but it is interesting to note that almost all other comments related to footpaths or access roads with no houses facing onto them. The map in Figure 7.9 is an attempt to summarise these locations. Places that were specifically mentioned are shown either as a line to indicate a route or by hatching. In addition to specifically named places there are many references to alleyways, footpaths around schools and to wooded areas, underpasses, dark areas, lonely areas, e.g. garage blocks, and paths out of sight of roads (see photo below). Of particular interest is the reason given for disliking these places. Lighting was often not working and it often took weeks to be repaired once reported (McDonnell, 2000). The map in Figure 7.9 also shows, in hatching, the locations from which respondents to the questionnaire report illegal drug sales taking place.

Important lessons emerge from these findings. Residents do not see the areas around houses as a primary source of fear or anxiety about safety. The locations of fear are on the segregated system of pedestrian footpaths that cover this area of housing, and primary access roads without houses. It follows from this that it is the design of the neighbourhood that is contributing to fear of crime. It is the original design policy that required a segregated pedestrian network of footpaths to give access to local shops, schools and transport that is responsible for fear of crime. The problems of maintenance of lighting and the lack of maintenance of landscape planting that had become badly overgrown were a further cause of this deterioration of the estate.

The lighting research that has been done over the past decade or so (much of it by Kate Painter – see, for example, Painter, 1994; Painter and Farrington, 1997 – and Pease, 1999) has made the case for improving street lighting on run-down council estates and elsewhere. However, lighting does not seem to be an adequate solution to the long-term faults in design policy. Surely the focus should be on getting new developments right in the first place. The ideal approach should be to:

Design principal pedestrian routes to follow streets with houses and not along the backs of houses, through segregated pedestrian underpasses, or open or wooded areas etc.

View of part of the segregated pedestrian network showing an underpass on the Blackthorn estate

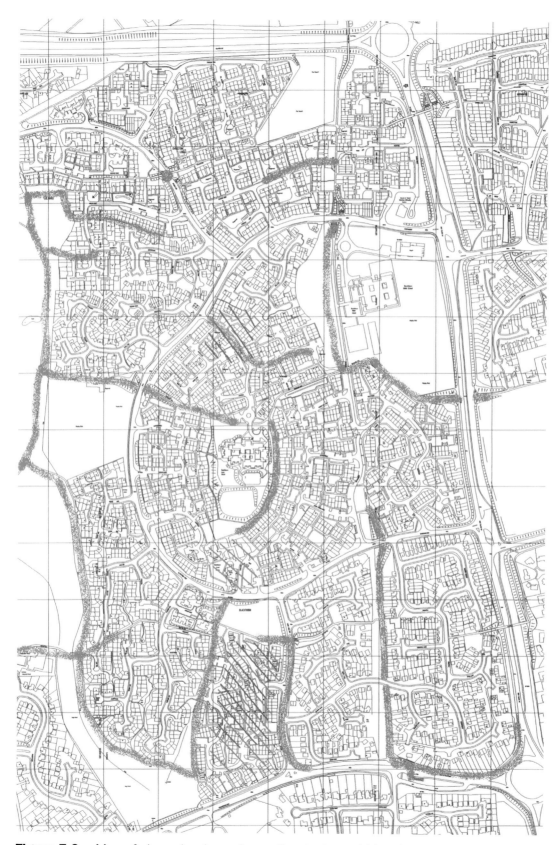

Figure 7.9   Map of places local people say they try to avoid (marked by bold lines and hatchings)

The question of lighting would then simply be a matter of lighting streets to a good standard. Personal observation of recent housing developments leads the author to believe that there is an argument for much more quality and contextual thinking in the lighting of streets. It is not so much a question of raising the level of illumination. New residential streets with no front gardens (just footpaths and roadways between houses) can be far too brightly lit when all houses are painted white, cream, pink or pale green.

Case studies

This chapter presents three case studies. They were chosen to illustrate typical forms of modern housing development. However, with fast-changing fashion in housing design it is impossible to illustrate substantial crime experience of developments built and occupied in very recent design styles because it may take five or six years from design to completion and full occupation of an estate. The case studies chosen are two conventional housing developments designed about the same time that *Crime Free Housing* was published in the early 1990s and a more recent design in the new urban style.

In assembling crime data for these three case studies, a neighbouring area of older and differently designed housing was included as a comparison area. It is not the absolute levels of crime that were of interest so much as how they compared with neighbouring areas. In the event, for all three studies the comparison areas turned out to be as interesting as the case study areas. The case studies were as follows:

1. *Cul-de-sac system with no footpaths* – to confirm that linking footpaths are probably the main weakness of modern suburban housing development. The comparison area is neighbouring public sector housing from the 1950s.

2. *Cul-de-sac systems but with a highly permeable pedestrian network* – it was believed that the mini pedestrian linking streets with bollards might provide a more permeable and walkable neighbourhood (see page 25 of *Better places to live*, DTLR/CABE, 2001). The comparison area is a small development of social housing.

3. *New urban style of suburban development* – houses are built to the edge of the sidewalk. The streets are all through streets and there is a small square mimicking a traditional town. The comparison area is made up of two cul-de-sac systems of older housing developments (probably early 1980s), one of which includes several small mews cul-de-sacs, after designs proposed in the Essex Design Guide (first version, 1973).

Case Study 1. Cul-de-sac system without footpaths

This development was built between 1995 and 1998 by a well known national house-builder. The houses are detached but modestly sized for the upper-middle-income market. The 65 houses all have garages and front driveways, the fronts are open-planned and mainly grassed. There is a side gate at the front leading to each back garden. The roadway is a branching cul-de-sac ending in shared carways. The site was used previously as an industrial laboratory and had only one entrance. This was retained as it fitted the hilly landform. The site had a group of historically valuable trees, the remains of landscaping around an earlier 19th-century house. The side boundaries are parkland to the east, an ancient lane giving access to other housing developments to the north and the other two sides back onto existing back gardens. The edge along the lane on the north side is defined by a very high retaining wall to accommodate the hilly nature of the site.

The area for comparison was taken as two roads from the neighbouring development to the north built in the 1950s in a style common to new town development of the time. It contains 113 dwellings – 24 flats in four blocks of three-storey flats overlooking the parkland area on the brow of the hill, and 89 terraced houses with back alleys to give access to gardens. Provision for cars was intended to be in banks of garages in garage courts, which can be easily recognised in the accompanying maps. Also there is a well-established pattern of street parking on this neighbouring estate.

Findings

Police sources generously provided data for the period 1995–2002, that is from the beginning of the case study development. On examination, it was clear that there was sufficient crime data to concentrate only on those years when the development was virtually complete. The data in Table 8.1 shows an analysis of all crime on the estate for 1998–2001. There may have been some minor finishing work on the estate in 1998 but by then all houses had been occupied. The table also shows crime occurring in the comparison area during the same period, and a map of this crime distribution is shown in Figure 8.1. It should be noted that the mapping of crime is approximate, but it is based on a printout from the police computerised map references and so it is a fair representation of the pattern.

Table 8.1 Crime recorded by the police for Case Study 1 area for the period 1998–2001

Crime type	1998	1999	2000	2001	Total
CASE STUDY 1 (65 houses)					
Burglary of a dwelling	0	2	0	0	2
Burglary other	0	0	0	0	0
Theft of cars	0	2	0	0	2
Theft from cars	0	1	0	0	1
Criminal damage to cars	0	0	0	0	0
Interference with cars	0	0	0	0	0
Criminal damage to a dwelling	0	0	0	0	0
Other criminal damage	0	0	0	0	0
Theft of bicycle	0	0	0	0	0
Other thefts	0	0	0	0	0
Case Study 1 totals	0	5	0	0	5
COMPARISON AREA 1 (New Town) (89 terraced houses and 24 flats)					
Burglary of a dwelling	3	0	1	2	6
Burglary other	1	1	1	0	3
Theft of cars	0	1	2	2	5
Theft from cars	5	3	1	3	12
Criminal damage to cars	1	4	2	2	9
Interference with cars	0	0	0	0	0
Criminal damage to a dwelling	0	1	0	2	3
Other criminal damage	0	1	0	0	1
Theft of bicycle	2	0	0	0	2
Other thefts	0	0	0	1	1
Comparison area totals	12	11	7	12	42

Crime rate for Case Study 1 is 19 crimes/1000 households/year
Crime rate for the comparison area is 93 crimes/1000 households/year

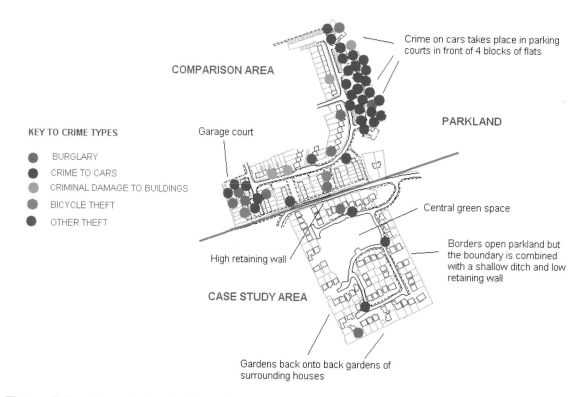

KEY TO CRIME TYPES

- BURGLARY
- CRIME TO CARS
- CRIMINAL DAMAGE TO BUILDINGS
- BICYCLE THEFT
- OTHER THEFT

COMPARISON AREA

Crime on cars takes place in parking courts in front of 4 blocks of flats

PARKLAND

Garage court

Central green space

Borders open parkland but the boundary is combined with a shallow ditch and low retaining wall

High retaining wall

CASE STUDY AREA

Gardens back onto back gardens of surrounding houses

Figure 8.1 Map of crime in Case Study 1 – approximate locations of crimes for 1998–2001

The first point to note is that the case study area is a low-crime area compared with the high-crime comparison area. The overall crime rates are 19 and 93 crimes/1000 households/year. So the first conclusion is that although the case study area has only a low-crime level, there is the potential for crime in this area of the town. It cannot be argued that this new development is a long way from crime hot spots, nor that local criminals live too far away to commit crime here.

What makes the difference between these two areas? Socio-economically there is an obvious difference. The case study area is populated by upwardly mobile and generally young families often with two cars. The comparison estate will be a mixture of a long-established community of new town settlers, younger families and single people with generally lower income levels. Cars will be older and so more vulnerable to crime.

However, these socio-economic differences are reflected in the most concrete way by fundamental differences in the design of the housing. Leaving the blocks of flats to one side, the two developments have contrasting house forms. The case study site has detached houses with side gates to back gardens. Most houses face onto the street and across to houses opposite. The comparison new town houses are terraced with rear access to back gardens. Although many houses face the street, few houses face other houses across the street. The only situations where houses face each other is onto small greens at right-angles to the road or in a parking court in the southwest corner of the comparison area.

In relation to car crime (all motor vehicle crime involved cars), again the differences are fundamental. All houses in the case study area have space for two cars (at least) to park on the front private driveway of the house. There is very little street parking. In the comparison area, there are no private driveways. This is because even where terrace houses face a street, the space is inadequate or the levels of this hilly site make it impossible to construct a suitable driveway. There is some street parking but the predominant parking space is in the parking and garage courts shown on the map. It is not surprising to see from the table that car crime accounts for two-thirds of the crime in the comparison area.

The above points are general comments about the overall picture, but there is another level of analysis that seems well worth exploring further. In the case study area the recorded crimes are the more serious types of crime – two burglaries and three car crimes, one of which involved the theft of a car. The comparison area not only has these more serious crimes but also the more petty crimes of theft and criminal damage. The impression given by these figures is that, not only is there more crime in the comparison area, but it is more embedded in the culture of the area. Crime is more frequent and seems to be continuing at much the same level. It might be described as endemic.

The information we have about the case study area is quite different in character. Here there is no recorded petty crime and what crime there is was only reported in 1999. Since then there has been no more crime recorded. Here crime has not become endemic but it seems to have 'cured' itself. Of course, this is only a very small sample and only a short period in time, but it suggests a mechanism that seems of crucial importance if true.

This mechanism was suggested in the findings from 'Fifteen years on' – that safe designs get safer. What appears to have happened in this case study is that once the development was complete, some attempts were made to commit crime, but after a few incidents by perhaps one or two local offenders, they seem to have given up on the estate. It did not work out as a place for easy pickings and so the local criminal community abandoned it. If this idea is correct, then it is a very reassuring message.

Conclusion

What makes this case study development safe seems simple and in line with the findings from earlier chapters. It reinforces the view that:

A true cul-de-sac system (only one way in and out) is potentially safe because offenders have to make a conscious effort to go in. This of course only works where the social structure assumes that offenders are most likely to come from outside; it might not work for a different resident population.

The houses are themselves safe because:

Houses face each other across the street, have well supervised private drives and garages and gated access to all back gardens.

These are the basics that work even though there will be some weak points. These include the problem of odd corner houses being less well overlooked and the fact that the gates to the back garden are not full height and are of a light slatted construction with no lock or inside bolt.

Typical view of Case Study 1

Case Study 2: Cul-de-sac with footpaths

This second case study is in the same new town as Case Study 1. It was built at the same time and completed to much the same timetable. Unlike the first study two different developers were involved. The 154 houses vary more in price range from houses designed to be 'affordable' to houses of the upper-middle price bracket similar to those in Case Study 1. Some are in small terraces, some semi-detached and some detached.

The roadway is a cul-de-sac system, but there are wide access lanes linking the ends of the cul-de-sacs though blocked to vehicle movement by bollards. Two major features are an open green on the south-western side of the case study site which acts as a buffer between the case study and the comparison area. There is also a major pedestrian route running through the middle of the site linking a commercial area comprising supermarket, fast-food outlets and evening entertainment to other residential areas (see line on map in Figure 8.2). This route is also blocked to car movement by bollards but has a lot of pedestrian and some motorcycle traffic. There have been complaints about licensing issues by residents due to late evening disturbances by inebriated youths wending their way home along this route.

The comparison area has 52 houses and was chosen simply because it was a convenient adjacent area of relatively recent housing. It was built as affordable housing by a housing association. No details of this organisation were obtained but since it turns out to have more problems than expected, it may be that further investigation of this area would be of interest but is not covered by this study. The main purpose of the comparison is to show that (as with Case Study 1) there is crime in the neighbourhood around the case study site.

Together the whole case study area and its comparison area illustrate cul-de-sac development, in terms of vehicle access, while providing a highly permeable network of pedestrian movement. The only areas that are relatively inaccessible are the two small cul-de-sacs on the north-east edge of the site.

Findings

An analysis of the crime in the case study area and comparison area is shown in Table 8.2 and a map of the crime distribution is given in Figure 8.2. Both the case study area and the comparison area have higher overall crime rates than Case Study 1. The case study area has a rate of 45 crimes/1000 households/year while the comparison area crime rate rises to 168/1000 households/year. These figures are both roughly twice the levels for Case Study 1. Perhaps the most obvious general explanation for this is the proximity of both developments to the through pedestrian route that certainly attracts young males onto the site.

Beyond this rather superficial analysis there are several quite distinct points to make about the distribution of crime in the map in Figure 8.2. The first point is that the north-eastern edge of the development has no crime. These houses are very similar to those in the first case study – detached with garages, private drives, open fronts and a front gate to secure back gardens. Many of these houses are in two short cul-de-sacs.

The main crime problem for the remainder of the case study area is car crime (mainly theft from cars). All these crime sites are on pedestrian routes around the estate, especially in two clusters where there is shared street and communal parking bays for groups of smaller, lower-priced terraced houses, with neither garages nor private drives. It is easy to see how these areas might be targeted by youths wandering around the estate, first out of curiosity, and then, once these groups of less well supervised cars are known about, to thieve.

It is interesting that the provision for these grouped parking areas is a common solution in low-cost/price housing. Designers believe that parking in small groups is safe providing there is surveillance from surrounding houses. They also believe that through pedestrian movement makes these arrangements even safer (see page 57 in *Better places to live,* DTLR/CABE, 2001). However, the pattern of car crime found in this data does not support this current design advice from government.

The only encouraging sign is the pattern of change over time. The car crime in this case study area focuses only on the first of the four years of the analysis. In 1998 there were 14 thefts from cars, one in 1999 and none since. This decay pattern is similar to that in Case Study 1. Could this be another example of designs being tested in the early years, but settling down as a crime-free area once the local criminal community realises that it is too risky and decides to target elsewhere?

The problems of the comparison area are much more serious. Although there are good and bad years there is no evidence of the problem of crime going away. Car crime is moderate here and probably due to a riskier design. All parking is in public and semi-public space in communal bays in the street or in parking strips in front of houses. There are no private drives nor garages.

The worst problem is criminal damage to dwellings. Bluntly, this is a large number of incidents of throwing stones at house windows and some damage to security lights, a satellite dish and the removal of fencing panels. Three incidents involve abuse of a front door – kicking it, banging on it

Table 8.2   Crime recorded by the police for Case Study 2 area 1998–2001 (4-year period)

Crime type	1998	1999	2000	2001	Totals
CASE STUDY 2 (154 houses)					
Burglary in a dwelling	0	1	1	0	2
Burglary other	0	0	2	0	2
Theft of cars	0	0	0	0	0
Theft from cars	14	1	0	0	15
Criminal damage to cars	0	1	1	0	2
Interference with cars	0	0	1	0	1
Criminal damage to a dwelling	0	1	1	0	2
Other criminal damage	1	0	0	0	1
Theft of bicycle	0	0	1	0	1
Other theft	1	0	0	1	2
Case Study 2 totals	16	4	7	1	28
COMPARISON AREA 2 (social housing) (52 houses)					
Burglary in a dwelling	0	2	0	0	2
Burglary other	0	0	0	0	0
Theft of cars	0	0	2	0	2
Theft from cars	2	3	1	0	6
Criminal damage to cars	1	3	0	1	5
Interference with cars	0	0	0	0	0
Criminal damage to a dwelling	1	1	9	2	13
Other criminal damage	0	3	0	0	3
Theft of bicycle	0	1	1	1	3
Other theft	0	1	0	0	1
Comparison area totals	4	14	13	4	35

Crime rate for Case Study 2 is 45 crimes/1000 households/year

Crime rate for the comparison area is 168 crimes/1000 households/year

Figure 8.2   Map of crime in Case Study 2 for 1998–2001

and pushing the security viewer in with a stick. There is one report of a window broken by an airgun pellet. Reading through the limited descriptions made available, it looks as if some of this behaviour is nasty victimisation or harassment by children or young males from close by. For us to understand this crime pattern more fully would need a fuller investigation by police officers.

Nevertheless, there is every reason to believe that the design and layout of the area does make some contribution to the problem. Each of the streets involved in these criminal damage incidents is highly escapable. The three streets empty into a neutral pedestrian network enabling any offender (toerag is perhaps the more appropriate term) to run off and be out of sight in a few moments.

This problem of criminal damage reflects very accurately the finding in the main Northampton study about criminal damage. There, windows and doors were damaged when houses faced onto open green areas. It was assumed that these were areas that attracted youths and children to play and lark about. There is some similarity in this case study due to the readily observed presence of children and the character of the streets which have become a semi-vandalised improvised playground. But the real point in common is that both settings are highly escapable. They are both closely linked to open space and a number of separate escape routes.

Another point of similarity between the Northampton study and this comparison area is the reporting of damage to houses, particularly broken glass in windows. Both are managed as rental property. Could this be seen as an incentive for reporting damage since the repairs are more likely to be covered under the landlord's responsibility if it is recorded as a crime? In an owner-occupied home, damage would be dealt with by the owner, possibly under an insurance policy but not necessarily processed as a crime.

Although this explanation was put forward in Chapter 6, closer reading of the data made available suggests that something more insidious than horseplay is at work – the incidents seem more like harassment than horseplay. After all, in the very early Harrow study we clearly identified racial harassment against Asian households. In this case study there is no evidence of a racial minority but maybe victimisation and intimidation were still involved.

Conclusions

In this case study, the levels of crime are too high to be acceptable and it is clear that design improvements might have made both areas safer. The problem is not burglary, even though the houses are more loosely planned in the comparison area and not always facing other houses, although all houses face onto the street and have reasonably secure back gardens. The two main problems are theft from cars and criminal damage to houses.

Theft from cars occurs where cars are parked in shared parking areas rather than on private drives, and on streets that are highly permeable to pedestrian movement (and escape).

Criminal damage also occurs in streets that are highly permeable to pedestrian movement and escape, but the problem seems to be made worse by other matters associated with intimidation and harassment.

Viewpoint 1:
A crime-free cul-de-sac

Viewpoint 2:
Wide linking streets or lanes for pedestrian use only

Viewpoint 3:
This shared parking area was the location of a cluster of thefts from cars

Case Study 3: New urban style

This new development in the style of the new urbanism was barely complete at the time of study. The photographs, taken in July and August 2002, show that the street and pavement surfaces are still to be finished. The houses mostly abut the pavement and are designed in a traditional Georgian and earlier country-town style. There is a small square at the centre (Photo 1). Modern requirements of parking are provided in back garage courts and individual gated car ports (Photo 2).

Photo 1 – 'Town square'

Photo 2 – Garage/car ports on the left

The case study site is located near to a large area of earlier suburban cul-de-sac development (circa 1980). It is characterised by the inclusion of short mews like cul-de-sacs similar to that diagrammed in the first edition of the Essex Design Guide as shown below (Essex County Council, 1973: 97). This seemed a useful opportunity to compare designs that were both *à la mode* at the time of building.

Sketch of a mews design from Essex Design Guide 1973, page 97.

Findings

The subject of the case study has 82 houses, mainly as short terraces and semi-detached houses. The comparison area is made up of two branching cul-de-sac systems with 122 and 384 houses respectively. It would have been possible to subdivide the larger cul-de-sac system should the data demand it, but, as will be seen, this was not necessary.

Unlike the previous two case studies, crime data was requested for the 12 months August 2001 to July 2002. It would be pointless covering a longer period because the case study development would not have been completed. As it is, some of the houses would not have been occupied during this time period. As with all other data in this report, the Data Protection Act requires that actual addresses were not provided, but crime was coded by street name. The crime categories included all those that seemed likely to be related to design following the analysis in the earlier part of this report. The data received from the police was as shown in Table 8.3 and mapped in Figure 8.3.

The result of this case study was surprising. Most of the crime is in the area which is the subject of the case study. The cul-de-sac areas have virtually no crime, even though they are much larger. There are few footpaths within any of these developments. The boundaries to the cul-de-sac developments have paths, but their influence on crime seems minimal.

Table 8.3 Crimes reported in Case Study 3 for mid-2001 to mid-2002

Type of crime	New urbanism	Cul-de-sac A	Cul-de-sac B
28. Burglary in a dwelling	0	0	0
30. Burglary in other building	3	0	0
39. Theft from the person	1	0	0
44. Theft of pedal cycle	0	0	0
45. Theft from vehicle	0	0	0
48. Theft of motor vehicle	0	0	0
49. Theft other	3	0	0
126. Vehicle interference	0	0	0
58A. Criminal damage to a dwelling	0	0	0
58B. Criminal damage to other building	0	3	0
58C. Criminal damage to a vehicle	1	0	0
58D. Other criminal damage	1	0	0
Totals	9	3	0

Crime rate for Case Study 3 (New Urbanism) was 107 crimes/1000 households/year

Crime rate for Cul-de-sac A was 8 crimes/1000 households/year

Crime rate for Cul-de-sac B was 0 (zero) crime/1000 households/year

The next observation greatly supports the importance of Chapter 6 on theft and damage outside the home. All the crimes fit into this category. There were **no house burglaries and no car theft**. The research officer who provided the information confirmed this by telephone, and also indicated that the three incidents of criminal damage in 'Cul-de-sac A' were of damage to garages.

CASE STUDY AREA

● BURGLARY OTHER ● CRIMINAL DAMAGE OF CAR
● THEFT FROM PERSON ● CRIMINAL DAMAGE (PROBABLY A TREE)
● THEFT OTHER ● CRIMINAL DAMAGE OF BUILDING
(probably garages)

Figure 8.3 Crime plotted (approximately) in the three zones of the case study – the new urbanism is in blue

Those anxious about the implications of these findings – that the new urbanism may have more crime problems than cul-de-sac developments – can shelter behind the possibility that the crime pattern recorded in the new urbanist design may be unreliable. It might be that some of the burglary and theft was related to lack of security associated with building activity. However, the result does draw attention to the outbuildings and theft from the houses that are serviced through rear yards. Photo 3 shows the street at the back of these houses. The high gates provided for access to these yards are clearly a weak point in security. Not only might these gates be left insecure, especially when shared between properties, but also, as one police architect liaison officer pointed out on seeing this photograph, a handy lamp post has been placed close to the wall, to help any intending criminal to climb over.

Photo 3 – Gates to rear yards on the right

Conclusions

This new urban style of design has obvious visual appeal, and it certainly provides generally good surveillance and movement in the street. This case study cannot give a definitive view of the future crime risk of these new approaches to design, but it raises the possibility that new problems may arise in the servicing of these new styles of housing layout. There is no house burglary and only one vehicle-related crime, but it is the crimes in spaces in and around the housing that remain unresolved.

However, as experience shows in Chapter 7 there may be aspects of security that reduce on gradual maturity of the development and allow residents to adapt to these problems. We can only wait and see whether these crime patterns become more serious or simply fade with maturity. However, **we have been warned!**

The aim of the research reported in *Crime Free Housing* was to address the issue of crime in low-rise, largely suburban housing. By the early 1980s it was generally recognised that many of the high- and medium-rise public housing estates had problems of crime and vandalism and this had led to housing authorities abandoning that kind of development. It was assumed that most new housing would consist of conventional houses with at least some private garden or yard, and that this was likely to be the predominant form for dwellings for the foreseeable future. That assumption proved correct and we have seen continued low-rise housing development for the private sector and social housing. Also, through this period we have seen more and more high-rise public-sector housing of the 1960s being demolished.

By the end of the 1990s we have seen a change of emphasis towards mixed-use urban regeneration and the need to build on brownfield rather than greenfield sites with higher densities demanded by government policy. This will change the balance of property built for residential use to include more apartment building and other housing forms, but the basic need for more houses with external private space (gardens) will still be a major element in new housing development. If anyone has doubts about this they only have to examine the current trends in the opening and expansion of garden centres and the popularity of gardening programmes on television to see that the 'room outside' continues to be highly desirable as part of the home.[1]

No doubt some may feel that low-rise housing has little to do with crime, but the research on a provincial town such as Northampton and a London suburb like Harrow disprove this. Indeed, the levels of crime in some parts of the study area were quite high and became high-profile problem areas. It is also interesting to find in the case studies that relatively high crime areas do exist and need to be understood if we wish to create a low-crime society.

The original intention of *Crime Free Housing* was to show that residential crime can be controlled by design without having to rely on an excessive use of conventional security devices such as locking hardware or alarm systems. This report has reviewed the findings of the original study and other research that has since emerged to conclude that the original findings and proposal remain little challenged. The one area that has attracted controversy is over the question about cul-de-sac road layouts versus through-street, grid-like layouts.

The 'End of the road for the cul-de-sac' campaign that emerged from Hillier and Shu's work (2000) was seen as good news for those in the urban design movement who were pressing for the return of more traditional street forms as a way to bring life back into urban areas – the urban renaissance. An early example of this approach is in the guide to the rebuilding of Hulme in Manchester, which explicitly states 'The cul-de-sac is anti-urban in that it reduces permeability and legibility, promoting isolation not integration and, on the whole, will not be permitted' (Hulme Regeneration Limited, 1994).

Research from the reworking of the Northampton data does give some support to the idea that housing areas with through-streets and grid-like street patterns have lower crime rates for some burglary, car theft, theft from cars and some thefts from around the home. This is certainly good evidence that through-streets are generally good for crime, but can we go the whole way and condemn the cul-de-sac in housing development?. There is an alternative view that points out that it is only when cul-de-sacs are linked to a footpath network that they are associated with crime. Pure

1. *Room Outside* is the title of a book by landscape designer John Brooks. Published in 1968 by Thames & Hudson (London) it was then described as 'a new approach to garden design'.

cul-de-sacs have few crime problems, particular in middle-income housing. All three case studies in Chapter 8 support this position, showing that it is only if cul-de-sacs are linked by footpaths or similar connections to open space that they become a crime problem.

The reason for elaborating this point is that when the issue of cul-de-sacs versus through-streets is viewed in the context of a study of all residential crime in a wide range of layout settings, its significance is seen as less critical. It is clear from this report that any safe housing area is safe because it has a set of characteristics that work together to prevent specific crimes, not just because of one factor alone. For example, in all three case studies, there were areas of housing without burglary that could be described as follows:

Detached houses that face onto the street and have back gardens backing onto other gardens and a gated access at the side of the house to the rear. It is not essential that all houses face other houses and it does not matter whether the street is a cul-de-sac or not. However, it would be helpful to avoid the street being connected to an open network of segregated pedestrian routes suitable for escaping from the area unseen.

A study of guidance literature, not just crime prevention or security guidance but also more general design guides for urban and residential development, reveals a tendency for very loose and generalised statements, presumably intended to avoid being too prescriptive and allow designers some freedom for creative design solutions. The following example in one government publication identifies one of the principal means of crime prevention as:

Natural surveillance: neighbours should be able to see each other's houses, and where cars are parked (at front or back), owners should be able to see them.

No doubt some will see this statement (not attributed here to avoid criticism) as perfectly acceptable and helpful to a layout designer. Certainly natural surveillance is an important technique in designing out crime, but this statement is not seen as helpful when it is pointed out that there are plenty of descriptions of high-crime areas where the statement is also true.

The 12 requirement statements in *Crime Free Housing* (see Appendix 3) were an attempt to be more prescriptive and drive home the point that quite specific design features seemed to be capable of reducing crime risk. Although this list of requirements can be revised in the light of further analysis and other research discussed particularly in Chapter 4, it remains largely valid. However, despite the availability of this list of requirements for more than a decade it has never been accepted as a serious basis for designing out residential crime in any official guidance or practice-based literature.

The more one reflects on the weaknesses of the guidance produced for architects and planners and for the house-building industry as a whole, it becomes clear that there is a lack of insight into the purpose or function of the advice presented. Almost without exception guidance lacks clarity about which crimes are prevented by specific guidance statements.

This pattern goes right back to the influential Jane Jacobs and Oscar Newman. Jane Jacobs' impressive attack on Le Corbusier's planning ideas led to very simplistic ideas about prevention and the basis of safety of city sidewalks being 'eyes on the street'. Her interest was in safety from personal attacks, but her concept of 'eyes on the street' has been applied to all crime (Jacobs, 1961). Oscar Newman's theory of 'defensible space' is derived from analyses of crimes ranging from 'lingering' to murder and rape. There is no distinction in the crimes that 'defensible space' can prevent, it is offered almost as a panacea.

Perhaps the most important point made in *Crime Free Housing* is that it presents a much fuller picture of the crimes that are preventable through design. It is clear from this report that the problem is not just a question of preventing 'crime' or even 'burglary' but it is a series of tasks of preventing thieves breaking into your house, keeping your car safe and ensuring that items that are kept outside or in sheds or garages are safe. We also want to avoid being targets of malicious damage to our property.

In the hope of encouraging designers (and their clients) to take a more 'crime-specific' approach to designing out crime in housing development, it is proposed that issues of crime should be incorporated into the process of design and layout as part of the central functional design programme (design brief). Rather than turn the guidance on crime prevention into some kind of regulatory standard, as has been done with, for example, fire regulations, it should be seen as a set of functional requirements.

It is suggested that in developing new designs and layouts for any new housing development, designers and layout planners should be expected to work out a design strategy for each of the principal crime problems:

1. Burglary – a strategy to discourage people trying to break into the house.

2. Car crime – a strategy for providing a safe place to park cars.

3. Theft around the home – a strategy for protecting the front of the house, and items in gardens, sheds and garages.

4. Criminal damage – a strategy to minimise malicious damage to property.

Defining the task of design this way around puts the responsibility for thinking about these issues onto the planner or designer. It also opens the way to a more design-oriented approach than a prescriptive approach, giving designers more opportunity for flexibility in developing or adapting solutions that fit well with all other aspects of the design.

The following paragraphs attempt to summarise the findings from the report in terms of the four strategies that are required for the design and planning of any housing development. Rather than simply listing recommendations, an attempt has been made to put the various design recommendations into context.

1. Strategy to avoid house burglary

The strategy will usually have three parts. There is the question of how areas are targeted. There is the management of the threshold between the public street and the private interior of the house, and the control of access to the house by other routes.

Inhibiting target selection of a house for burglary

Criminological studies indicate that the targeting of specific areas and specific houses is the result of a variety of search methods, depending on the level of sophistication of the burglar. There is evidence that restricting major traffic flows through residential areas does reduce the overall level of criminal activity by making the areas less well known to non-residents. **Major traffic routes should be kept away from residential development, allowing only light through traffic** (page 27).

There is strong evidence to suggest that the availability of pedestrian escape routes to less well-supervised places makes for an attractive target, particularly with a network of footpaths and open areas of land etc. to disappear into. **Avoid networks of separate pedestrian footpaths to unsupervised areas. It is better to use the street network for most pedestrian movement** (pages 31–2).

Protecting the front

The front entrance or front face of the house needs to be well supervised to discourage attempts at direct attack by burglars. Apart from the inherent strength of the door construction and locking mechanism (current standards from British Standards or from the police Secured by Design scheme should be quite adequate for this purpose), security in residential areas comes from the risk to a potential burglar of being seen knocking to check that the house is unoccupied and perhaps attempting to force the door or break the lock in some manner.

The most effective design form to aid surveillance of the front of a house is the way it relates to the windows and front doors of other neighbouring houses. **Houses planned facing each other and close to neighbours on either side** are more likely to enable neighbours to casually watch their neighbour's houses (pages 32–3).

There is also some advantage in reducing burglary to **introduce some light through movement of traffic and make streets through-streets** to help bring some activity and presence of people into residential streets. Some streets in a residential area should be designed to carry light through traffic (page 27).

There is some evidence to suggest that a more ordered frontage on the street makes it easier to avoid weak points in potential access to the back of the house and easier to give surveillance to entry points (including side access). **Designers should be encouraged to take advantage of the principle of more enclosure and continuity advocated in some urban design guides** (pages 33–4),

The front door of the house needs to be clearly visible to pedestrians and drivers moving along the street, and so **avoid trees, shrubs and other potential obstructions developing to obscure the door and any other entry point at the front of house**. This might be achieved by reducing the depth of any front garden to a minimum and/or paving the area in front of these entry points to prevent excessive planting (page 34).

There is some limited evidence to suggest that houses with **front gardens that have low boundary walls or fences** are slightly better protected against burglary (involving heavier stolen goods). It may be that burglars feel more exposed if they can be seen moving to or from a gateway to the street (page 35).

Protecting the back of the house

Once the front of the house is protected, the strategy will need to consider protecting access to other sides of the house. If the house is a corner house it will effectively have two fronts. More normally burglars find it easier to enter a house from the back garden where they can work unobserved.

The task is to create a secure back garden or yard. The minimum enclosure is a full-height (of a man) fence, but designers should not be discouraged from using higher and more robust structures. Outbuildings are also a valuable barrier if incorporated into the garden boundary and are not easily climbed.

Consideration should be given to the possibility of offenders climbing fences from open or wasteland and from little used driveways or footpaths. **The best way to avoid this is for gardens to be planned back to back and side by side**. Where this cannot be done the use of higher fences or perhaps a more ornamental brick wall could be considered. Sloping landforms, ditches, banking, retaining walls and appropriate planting can all help improve the security of rear boundaries (page 37).

Access to the back garden is best provided through a lockable gate at the front of the house. It should be at the front and not recessed to promote good surveillance. It needs to be robust, at least as high as any fencing and provided with a strong keyed lock. If there is a strong case for entry from the side or rear much greater care should be given to considering the problems of security. For example, a robustly locked gate in a high brick wall might be satisfactory, especially if it is clearly in view from many windows. The habit of designers providing flimsy slatted gates for a back garden entry from a back path with no locking mechanism is a recipe for failure (page 37).

2. Strategy for safe parking

It is recognised that the design of cars has improved in terms of security over the past decade, but cars are still stolen. New technical developments in car security tend to influence theft of cars rather than theft of contents or components from cars and so thefts from remain a more difficult problem to solve. Similarly, criminal damage to cars, unlike the other two categories, has been on the increase. There remains a real issue of protecting cars while parked at home.

The central issue that emerges from research is that there are dramatic differences in risk depending on what kind of parking is provided. The least safe is communal parking in housing, particularly where it is to the side or rear of housing terraces. Where street parking is the main option then this is also where most car crime will occur (see Table 5.1, page 39). **Rates of car theft and theft from cars are low when parking is predominantly on private driveways**. This preferred location probably only functions well **in streets lined with houses to provide mutual surveillance of private driveways** (see page 43).

The problem is that even on private driveways theft *from* cars and other interference or damage to cars can occur. It may be that only by parking in private garages or inside a gated yard (side drive, etc.) can complete protection be guaranteed.

The use of parking courts seems to be increasingly introduced in the new urban design style. In theory, these present a problem for potential car crime and they generate rear access to back gardens. The idea of mixing parking courts with houses opening onto the courts is an interesting development, but there is no suitable evidence to offer guidance as to whether it will work or not. This is the kind of refining research that could be usefully carried out now.

Other general layout factors have been found to support safer parking. Grid street patterns appear to be less at risk from thefts of cars than cul-de-sac patterns. Presumably, this only works when cars are parked in the street where some through traffic deters car thieves. A grid pattern probably makes little difference when cars are parked on the front driveways of houses or in some back parking court.

However, the evidence seems much clearer on the question of footpath networks. **Networks of segregated footpaths appear to increase the risk of theft of and from cars**. Footpaths enable potential thieves to explore an area looking for targets and in the case of theft from cars, provide easy escape routes, particularly if paths lead to open ground or other unsupervised areas. **The preferred route for pedestrian movement is to follow the street pattern so that pedestrian movement is generally overlooked by houses** (page 43).

3. Strategy for minimising theft around the home

It is clear from the crime analyses reported in previous chapters that there are several similar problems of theft from both front and back of the house and from outbuildings such as garages and sheds. Designers need to consider how to make homes more secure for all these household items from tools to garden furniture and from sports equipment to overflow freezer capacity. Similarly, the storage of motorbikes, bicycles and even mowers requires more careful consideration.

In an age when people have ever more interests in acquiring gadgets and equipment for leisure activity, and when transport policy encourages a return to cycling and perhaps light motorcycles, there is clearly a growing need for safe storage of these items.

Garages
Garages or similar outbuildings are to be encouraged in that they provide a valuable safe place for the storage of the above items. Indeed, many households with garages attached to their houses do not use garages to park cars, but they use them for storage, workshop DIY and other leisure activities.

To reduce the risk of thefts, **garages are best planned next to the house**. In this situation they require relatively little additional security beyond good quality proprietary garage doors and simple keyed locking. This arrangement will work best in a conventional street lined with houses facing the street as this provides some casual surveillance from surrounding houses (page 55).

Where designers wish to set the garage further back on the housing plot to reduce the front garden and yet provide ample parking space on a driveway to the garage, they need to consider the security implications of the driveway giving access to the rear of the house. This may require a set of gates at the front face of the building or some means of supervising the side access and the garage front.

Protecting the front of the house
There is some evidence that some houses along streets that are part of well-used routes to and from evening activities such as evening entertainment (pubs, entertainment facilities, sports events, transport services) do suffer from more theft and minor damage to front gardens. Although the evidence is not strong, there is a case **for a little more protection for houses along busier well-used pedestrian routes. It may be that a buffer area between the house and public sidewalk/street is required, perhaps with waist high iron railings or similar boundary treatment** (page 58).

There is a problem of thefts from doorsteps. While delivery of milk bottles may no longer be relevant to most modern life, the need to deliver items to the front door continues (for example through the growing use of Internet shopping). **The front of the house requires somewhere safe and out of sight to leave deliveries of all kinds including, parcels and mail-order post and milk or groceries** (page 58).

It seems sensible (but not obligatory) to consider combining this facility with servicing such as meter-reading.

A secure back yard

Apart from outbuildings such as a garage, the best strategy for providing safe places to leave bicycles, motorcycles, garden equipment and furniture or indeed items for which there may not be room inside is in a secure back garden or yard.

The best way to create a secure garden is to plan gardens back to back and side by side. This reduces the risk of thieves climbing fences (see also burglary strategy). Where this is not possible or practical, **it is important to ensure the boundary is high enough not to see into the garden from outside** even allowing for changing levels (pages 60–1)

Bicycles and motorcycles tend to be taken (other than from garages) from the front of the house and in the case of motorcycles even in the street or communal parking. The ideal strategy is to make it easy to leave bikes in a secure back yard. **The best way of providing for this is to provide a gated access from the front of the house to the back garden.** Perhaps consideration should be given to providing wide enough access to move larger items through as necessary. If only rear access is contemplated in smaller terraced housing much more care needs to be given to the problem of securing it (see also burglary strategy).

The effectiveness of any gate to the back garden will benefit from careful detailed design that uses self-closing mechanisms and proper key-operated locks rather than latches.

4. Strategy for avoiding criminal damage

The evidence about the problems of criminal damage to low-rise housing is not well developed, but there is sufficient to suggest that care should be taken when planning open green areas in front of housing frontages.

Where these spaces are likely to be used by children and youths some physical separation or buffer space should be considered. This might be achieved by using protective landscaping (e.g. sloping ground to discourage games) and/or the presence of a lightly used carriageway or even a well used pedestrian route (page 67).

Appendix 1

A classification of residential and non-residential crime

Crime data recorded for 1982 from Northampton (10% sample, N=1299) and five wards in the London Borough of Harrow (N=1508). All figures are given as percentages.

BURGLARY (includes some thefts in police records)	Harrow 1982	Northampton 1982
Residential burglary		
House burglary		
Luxury goods stolen	2.6	0.0
Electrical goods stolen	6.8	1.8
Cash and jewellery stolen	7.4	2.1
Failed attempted entries to dwelling	5.2	2.3
Trivial and other burglary	1.0	0.6
	23.0	**6.8**
Gas/electric meter broken opens		
Break-in to house suggesting outside offender	< 0.1	0.6
No break-in, occupants suspected	0.2	1.1
No break-in but occupants not suspected	0.2	1.8
	0.5	**3.5**
Aggravated burglary	0.1	0.0
Burglary with major damage	0.3	<0.1
Burglary of flats	0.5	0.4
Theft from garages and sheds	2.9	1.4
Total residential burglary	**27.3**	**12.2**
Non-residential burglary		
Shops	2.7	1.5
Smash and grab raids	0.5	0.5
Office or business premises	2.0	4.1
Commercial garages or workshops	0.3	0.3
Building site offices	0.5	> 0.1
Public houses	0.1	0.2
Service stations	0.1	> 0.1
School break-ins	1.2	1.7
Clubhouses/pavilions	1.1	0.5
Sheds for grounds staff	0.4	> 0.1
Health service premises	0.3	> 0.1
Caravans and tents	0.0	0.6
Other	0.8	0.6
Total non-residential burglary	**10.0**	**10.4**

THEFT (excludes vehicle crime)	Harrow 1982	Northampton 1982
Residential theft		
Inside the home		
By tricking people	0.3	0.2
By legitimate visitors	1.1	1.1
Theft in residential institutions	0.2	1.1
Outside the house		
Milk stolen from doorsteps	0.0	0.8
Clothes taken from washing lines	0.3	1.5
Items stolen from gardens	1.1	0.7
Bicycles	1.7	1.8
Other	0.3	0.2
Theft from communal areas of flats	0.1	0.4
Empty houses	0.2	>0.1
Total residential theft	**5.3**	**7.8**
Non residential theft		
In public places		
Pubs/discos/restaurants	0.3	0.8
Lockers and changing rooms	0.4	0.5
Forgotten purses and wallets subsequently stolen	0.3	0.4
Purses or cash taken from women shoppers	0.3	0.5
Pickpocketing	0.1	>0.1
Bicycles	1.6	3.1
Other	0.4	0.8
	3.4	**6.2**
Theft from a business		
Shoplifting	1.9	6.4
Non-payment for services	0.6	0.5
Theft from a building site	0.5	1.5
Theft by employees	0.6	0.8
Deliveries taken from outside premises	0.0	0.5
From employees	1.0	1.5
Outsiders stealing cash	0.3	>0.1
Theft from meters, coin boxes, vending machines	0.0	0.5
Other thefts from businesses	0.6	1.0
	5.5	**12.7**
Total non-residential theft	**8.9**	**18.9**

VIOLENT CRIME	Harrow 1982	Northampton 1982
Disputes in non-domestic context	1.7	2.8
Domestic violence	0.4	0.5
Assault and robbery in the street	0.4	0.2
Handbag snatches	0.2	0.3
Sexual assaults/incidents in public places	1.3	1.1
Other violence	0.5	0.5
Total violent crime	**5.0**	**5.3**

CRIMINAL DAMAGE (not motor vehicles)

Residential		
Rowdy youths	1.5	0.2
Victimisation of Asian households	2.5	0.0
Victimisation of other households	1.1	0.6
Air gun attacks	0.4	0.0
Arson	0.1	0.4
Other	0.3	0.2
	5.9	1.4

Non-residential		
Shop windows	1.7	1.2
Drunken/emotional incidents	0.7	0.5
School	0.4	0.5
Huts, site offices and pavilions	0.4	0.3
Fire setting	0.3	0.6
Other	0.8	0.9
	4.4	4.0

Total criminal damage	**10.3**	**5.4**

VEHICLE CRIME	Harrow 1982	Northampton 1982
Residential		
Theft of motor vehicles		
Cars	6.9	4.8
Motorcycles	1.1	1.3
Commercial vehicles	>0.1	0.0
	8.1	**6.2**
Theft from motor vehicles		
Property left in cars	5.6	3.7
External components from cars	1.1	0.6
Petrol siphoned from cars	0.3	0.7
Taking car batteries	0.3	0.2
Components from motorcycles	0.1	0.2
	7.4	**5.4**
Criminal damage to motor vehicles		
Car damage (reason unknown)	2.1	1.0
Car damage related to disputes	0.7	0.2
Car damage (possible racial motive)	0.7	0.0
Damage to other motor vehicles	>0.1	>0.1
	3.6	**1.3**
Total residential vehicle crime	**19.0**	**12.9**
Non-residential		
Theft of motor vehicles		
Cars	2.9	4.9
Motorcycles	>0.1	1.0
Commercial vehicles	0.4	0.3
	3.3	**6.2**
Theft from motor vehicles		
Property left in cars	3.1	3.5
From commercial vehicles	0.2	0.5
Components from motorcycles	>0.1	0.5
Petrol siphoned from motor vehicle	0.5	0.5
Removing batteries	0.0	0.2
Taking external components	0.3	>0.1
	4.2	**5.4**
Other vehicle theft	1.0	1.8
Malicious damage to motor vehicles	0.7	1.3
Total non-residential vehicle crime	**9.2**	**14.7**
OTHER RECORDED CRIME		
Possession of an offensive weapon	0.5	0.0
Deception	0.4	3.8
Receiving/handling	0.3	1.2
Other/ Insufficient information to classify	3.9	7.4
	5.1	12.4
	100%	**100%**

Appendix 2

Residential crime data

The following table contains the classification of data on residential crime used in the Harrow and Northampton studies for 1982 and for Northampton in 1987. The data are taken from the original unpublished research paper by Poyner, Helson and Webb (1985) and from *Crime Free Housing* (Poyner and Webb, 1991). The order of the two classifications is slightly amended to fit into the chapter structure of this report. The classification of malicious/criminal damage is different in the two sources because the 1987 data was less detailed due to limitations imposed by the Data Protection Act. There are also slight differences in the wording used in the two sources. The most clearly worded version is used here. Where information is not available (n/a) this means that the source records from which the 1987 data in *Crime Free Housing* was derived, have since been disposed of.

The crime sample for the 1987 data for the north-east area of Northampton was not drawn from all recorded crime as were the two samples for 1982. Only those categories of recorded crime thought relevant to the analysis for *Crime Free Housing* were assembled. For example, domestic violence, although a crime in a residential setting, was so small a recorded crime problem in the 1982 samples and unlikely to be influenced by housing layout that it was ignored in the 1987 study.

The purpose of providing this data is to give greater insight into the range of crimes that can be described as residential crime, and to indicate the relative sizes of the elements in the three samples. It is important to note that the differences in the two years for the Northampton data is not due simply to the growth in crime that was occurring at the time, but that the two samples are for completely different geographical areas. The 1982 data was a 10% sample for all of Northampton whereas the 1987 data was a 100% sample for the layout areas shown in Figure 3.2.

For a classification of all recorded crime see the analysis of 1982 data in Appendix 1.

Type of crime	1982 Harrow N	1982 Harrow N/1000	1982 N'pton N	1982 N'pton N/1000	1987 N'pton N	1987 N'pton N/1000
Residential burglary						
House burglary						
Luxury goods	39	2.3	0	0.0	8	0.6
Electrical goods	102	6.1	23	4.0	238	17.0
Cash and jewellery	111	6.6	27	4.7	103	7.4
Trivial	13	0.8	6	1.0	8	0.6
Aggravated burglary	2	0.1	0	0.0	2	0.1
Burglary involving major damage	4	0.2	1	0.2	1	0.1
Unsuccessful attempts	78	4.7	30	5.3	148	10.6
Other	3	0.2	2	0.4	10	0.7
Not yet known what was stolen	–	–	–	–	32	2.2
Total house burglary	352	21.0	89	15.6	550	39.3
Flats and residential institutions burglary	8	0.5	5	0.9	14	1.0
Coin meters						
Associated with a break-in	1	0.1	8	1.4	19	1.4
No signs of forced entry to dwelling	6	0.4	38	6.7	25	1.8
Total residential burglary	367	22.0	140	24.6	608	43.5
Vehicle crime (excludes motorcycles)						
Theft of motor vehicles (excl. motorcycles)						
Cars	105	6.3	63	11.0	295	21.1
Commercial vehicles	1	0.1	0	0.0	2	0.1
Total thefts of motor vehicles	106	6.4	63	11.0	297	21.2
Theft from motor vehicles (excl. motorcycles)						
Property left in cars	84	5.0	48	8.4	355	25.4
External car components	17	1.0	8	1.4	118	8.4
Petrol siphoned from cars	4	0.2	9	1.6	36	2.6
Car batteries removed	4	0.2	3	0.5	6	0.4
Property stolen from other vehicles[1]	–	–	–	–	15	1.1
Total theft from motor vehicles	109	6.4	68	11.9	530	37.9

Type of crime	1982 Harrow N	1982 Harrow N/1000	1982 N'pton N	1982 N'pton N/1000	1987 N'pton N	1987 N'pton N/1000
Malicious damage to motor vehicles[2]						
Cars (reason unknown)	84	5.0	48	8.4		
Cars (damaged during dispute)	11	0.7	3	0.5		
Cars (damage with racial motive)	11	0.7	0	0.0		
Damage to other motor vehicles	2	0.1	2	0.3		
Criminal damage to motor vehicles[2]						
Car windows smashed					24	1.7
Car bodywork damaged					23	1.6
Car tyres slashed					9	0.6
Other car damage					19	1.4
Damage to other vehicles					14	1.0
Damage but types of vehicle not recorded					25	1.8
Total criminal damage to motor vehicles	108	6.5	53	9.2	114	9.1
Thefts and damage around the home						
Thefts from garages					59	4.3
Thefts from garden sheds					36	2.6
Theft from garages and sheds	44	2.6	18	3.2	95	6.9
Theft outside the house:						
Milk, parcels, etc. taken from doorsteps[3]	–	–	11	1.9	25	1.8
Clothes from washing lines	5	0.3	19	3.3	25	1.8
Plants and garden ornaments stolen	16	1.0	9	1.6	17	1.2
Bicycles (from gardens and driveways)	26	1.6	23	4.0	56	4.0
Property taken from external meter boxes[2]	–	–	–	–	7	0.5
Other theft outside the house	4	0.2	3	0.5	27	1.9
Total theft outside the house	51	3.1	65	11.3	157	11.2
Malicious damage[2]						
Rowdy youths	22	1.3	3	0.5		
Victimisation:						
a. Asian households	37	2.2	–	–		
b. Other	17	1.0	8	1.4		
Air gun attacks	6	0.4	–	–		
Arson	2	0.1	5	0.9		
Other	5	0.3	2	0.3		

Type of crime	1982 Harrow N	1982 Harrow N/1000	1982 N'pton N	1982 N'pton N/1000	1987 N'pton N	1987 N'pton N/1000
Criminal damage in residential areas						
Stones and other objects through windows					68	4.9
Windows broken by airgun pellets					6	0.4
Other smashed windows					23	1.6
Door glass broken					16	1.1
Doors/windows forced					11	0.8
Garden fences, walls and gates damaged					24	1.7
Following an argument					16	1.1
Other damage to outside of houses					11	0.6
Other damage not to house or garage					10	0.7
Total of damage around the home	89	5.3	18	3.1	185	12.9
Theft of motorcycles	16	1.0	17	3.0	127	9.1
Theft of components from motorcycles	2	0.1	2	0.3	8	0.6
Total of motorcycle theft from around the home	18	1.1	19	3.3	135	9.7
TOTAL theft and damage around the home	202	12.1	120	20.9	572	52.7
Other residential crime						
Theft inside the home						
By tricking people	5	0.3	2	0.3	n/a	n/a
By legitimate visitors	16	1.0	14	2.5	n/a	n/a
From residential institutions	3	0.2	14	2.5	n/a	n/a
	24	1.5	30	5.3	102	7.3
Theft from communal areas in flats	2	0.1	5	0.9	n/a	n/a
Theft from empty houses	3	0.2	1	0.2	n/a	n/a
Domestic violence (low levels of reporting)	6	0.4	6	0.4	n/a	n/a

Notes

[1] This category was not used in 1982 analysis.

[2] Different classifications are given for criminal damage in the 1982 and 1987 data. The reason is simply that the detail available in the 1987 data was less than in 1982 due to computerisation and the limitations created by the Data Protection Act.

[3] Not recorded at that time in the Metropolitan Police area.

Appendix 3

'Summary of design requirements'

The 12 requirements proposed in *Crime Free Housing* are listed below for reference purposes (Poyner and Webb, 1991: viii–ix). These statements are greatly simplified and do not explain the arguments behind each recommendation. For fuller descriptions of these requirements see pages 97–101 of *Crime Free Housing*.

Although these requirements have been developed and modified in this report, layout designs conforming to this old set of guidance will still avoid most crime. The purpose of the modified guidance is not only to update the content in the light of further research and current design practice, but also to allow layout designers more freedom or flexibility in their design process.

Moderate locking security. Houses require only a moderate level of locking security provided the opportunity for crime is controlled by the design and layout of the housing area.

Facing windows. The front windows of houses should face each other across the street or similar shared access area to create a system of mutual surveillance.

High fences at the sides and rear. The side and rear boundaries of individual house plots should be provided with full-height fencing or walls.

Front access to a secure yard. There should be a gateway at the front of the house giving access to a secure yard or garden area. The gateway should be designed so that it can be locked or bolted on the inside and supervised from the inside of the house.

Access for services and deliveries. There should be a place to store waste bins and provide access to gas and electricity meters at the front of the house. It is also desirable to provide a place by the front door where deliveries can be left under cover and out of sight of the public footpath.

Space at the front. There seems to be a need for an area in front of the house between the house and public access areas.

On-curtilage hardstanding for cars. All car parking should be on hardstandings within the curtilage of the house, preferably at the front to facilitate surveillance.

A garage at the side of the house. Any garage should be provided at the side of the house, close to the front entrance.

Limit road access. It is an advantage to reduce the number of road access points to an area of housing and so avoid creating through-traffic routes.

Avoid through pedestrian routes. Where pedestrian routes are separate from the roadways, they should not be planned to create a series of through-routes connecting with other housing areas or open spaces.

Surveillance of access roads. Houses should be oriented to face access routes and especially to focus on points of entry into an area to provide intensive surveillance.

Green spaces outside housing areas. Green open spaces should be provided near the entrances to housing areas rather than within them.

References

Aldous, T., 1992. *Urban Villages*, Urban Villages Group, London.

Atlas, R. and W.G. LeBlanc, 1994 'Environmental barriers to crime', *Ergonomics in Design*, October, pp. 9–16.

Baldwin, J. and A.E. Bottoms, 1976. *The Urban Criminal*, Tavistock Publications, London.

Beavon, D.J.K., P.L. Brantingham and P.J. Brantingham, 1994. 'The Influence of Street Networks on the Patterning of Property Offenses', in R.V. Clarke (ed.), *Crime Prevention Studies, Vol. 2*. Criminal Justice Press, Monsey, New York.

Beckford, C., undated, (circa 1995). *The Alleygater's Guide*, Crime Prevention Design Adviser for the London Borough of Ealing, Metropolitan Police, London (Ealing Police Station).

Bennett, G., J. Noble and M. Jenks, 1984. *More than Just a Road*, Information Sheet 13, Department of the Environment, London.

Birkbeck, D., 2001. 'Architects workload survey', *RIBAJ*, August, pp. 68–71.

Blakely, E.J. and M.G. Snyder, 1998. 'Separate Places: Crime and Security in Gated Communities' in Felson, M. and R.B. Peiser (editors) *Reducing Crime Through Real Estate Development and Management*, Urban Land Institute, Washington, DC.

Brantingham P.L. and P.J. Brantingham, 1981. 'Notes on the Geometry of Crime' in P.J. Brantingham and P.L. Brantingham (eds), *Environmental Criminology*, Sage Publications, Beverly Hills. (Reissued in 1991 by Waveland Press, Prospect Heights, Illinois.)

British Standards Institution, 1986. *British Standard Guide for Security of Buildings against Crime* Part 1. Dwellings, BS 8220: Part 1: 1986 (since revised).

Budd, T., 1999. *Burglary of Domestic Dwellings – Finding from the British Crime Survey*, Home Office Statistical Bulletin, Home Office, London.

Coleman, A., 1985. *Utopia on Trial – Vision and Reality in Planned Housing*, Hilary Shipman, London.

Coleman, A., 1987. 'More Sensitive House-Design Criteria Please', *House Builder*, October, pp. 23–6.

Department of the Environment, 1994. *Planning Out Crime*, Circular 5/94, HMSO, London.

Department of the Environment, Transport and the Regions, 1998. *Places, Streets & Movement*, A companion guide to Design Bulletin 32 Residential roads and footpaths, Department of Environment, Transport and the Regions, London.

Department of the Environment, Transport and the Regions, 2000a. *Planning Policy Guidance Note 3: Housing*, The Stationery Office, London.

Department of the Environment, Transport and the Regions, 2000b. *By Design: Urban Design in the Planning System: Towards Better Practice*, available from Thomas Telford Publishing, London.

Department for Transport, Local Government and the Regions jointly with Commission for Architecture and the Built Environment, 2001. *Better places to live*, A companion guide to PPG3, HMSO, London (available through Thomas Telford, Kent).

Ekblom, P., H. Law and M. Sutton, 1996. *Safer Cities and Domestic Burglary*, Home Office Research Study 164, Home Office, London.

Essex County Council, 1973. *A Design Guide for Residential Areas*, Essex County Council, Chelmsford. Now revised as: Essex Planning Officers' Association, 1997. *The Essex Design Guide for Residential and Mixed Use Areas*, Essex County Council.

Evans, D.J. and M. Fletcher, 1998. 'Residential Burglary within an Affluent Housing Area' *International Journal of Risk, Security and Crime Prevention,* 3(3): 181–91.

Fairs, M. 1998. 'End of the road for the cul-de-sac', *Building Design*, 13 November.

Fowler, F.J. Jr. and T.W. Mangione, 1982. *Neighbourhood Crime, Fear and Social Control: A Second Look at the Hartford Program*, US Department of Justice, National Institute of Justice, Washington, DC.

Ham-Rowbottom, K.A., R. Gifford and K.T. Shaw, 1999. 'Defensible Space Theory and the Police: Assessing the Vulnerability of Residences to Burglary', *Journal of Environmental Psychology*, 19(2): 117–29.

Hampshire, R. and M. Wilkinson, 1999. *Youth Shelters and Sports Systems*, Thames Valley Police.

Hill, N. 1986. *Prepayment Coin Meters: A Target for Burglary*, Crime Prevention Unit Paper 6, Home Office, London.

Hillier, B. and S.C.F. Shu, 2000. 'Crime and Urban Layout: The Need for Evidence', in S. Ballintyne, K. Pease and V. McLaren (eds), *Secure Foundations: Key Issues in Crime Prevention, Crime Reduction and Community Safety*, Institute for Public Policy Research, London.

Home Office, 1988. *Criminal Statistics England and Wales 1987*, HMSO, London.

Hulme Regeneration Limited, 1994. *Rebuilding the City: A Guide to Development in Hulme*, Hulme City Challenge, Manchester.

Jacobs, J., 1961. *The Death and Life of Great American Cities: The Failure of Town Planning*, Random House. (First published in Britain by Jonathan Cape in 1962. Also in Penguin Books.)

Kershaw, C., T. Budd, G. Kinshott, J. Mattinson, P. Mayhew and A. Myhill, 2000 *The 2000 British Crime Survey*, Home Office Statistical Bulletin 18/00, Home Office, London.

Llewelyn-Davies, 2000. *Urban Design Compendium*, English Partnerships/The Housing Corporation, London.

MacDonald, J.E. and R. Gifford, 1989. 'Territorial Cues and Defensible Space Theory: The Burglar's Point of View', *Journal of Environmental Psychology* 9(3): 193–205.

McDonnell, M. 2000. 'A Survey of Residents' Views on Crime and Disorder in the Blackthorn Area 1999', in-house report, Northampton Community Safety Partnership (Northampton Borough Council, Northampton County Council and Northamptonshire Police).

Maguire, M. and T. Bennett, 1982. *Burglary in a Dwelling: The Offence, The Offender and the Victim*, Heinemann, London.

Mawby, R.I., 2001. *Burglary*, Willan Publishing, Cullompton, Devon.

Methven, A., 2001. *Briefing Notes on Community Safety Projects*, Northampton Community Safety Partnership (Northampton Borough Council, Northampton County Council and Northamptonshire Police).

National House-Building Council, 1986. *NHBC Guidance on How the Security of New Homes Can Be Improved*, NHBC, London.

Nee, C. and M. Taylor, 1988. 'Residential Burglary in the Republic of Ireland: A Situational Perspective', *Howard Journal*, 27(2): 105–16.

Newman, O., 1973. *Defensible Space: People and Design in the Violent City*, Architectural Press, London. (Published in US by Macmillan in 1972).

Newman, O., 1980. *Community of Interest*, Anchor Press/Doubleday, Garden City, New York.

Noble, J. and M. Jenks, 1989. *Safety and Security in Private Sector Housing Schemes: A Study of Layout Design Considerations*, The Housing Research Foundation: National House-Building Council, Amersham, Bucks.

Noble, J. and A. Smith, 1992. *Design Bulletin 32 – Residential roads and footpaths: layout considerations* (second edition), Departments of Environment and Transport, HMSO, London.

Noble, J., K. Elvin and R. Whitaker, 1977. *Design Bulletin 32 – Residential roads and footpaths: layout considerations*, Departments of Environment and Transport, HMSO, London.

Painter, K., 1994. 'The Impact of Street Lighting on Crime, Fear and Pedestrian Street Use', *Security Journal* (July).

Painter, K., 1999. *A Guide for Crime and Disorder Reduction through a Public Lighting Strategy*, Institution of Lighting Engineers, Rugby, Warwickshire.

Painter, K. and D. Farrington, 1997. 'The Crime Reducing Effect of Improved Street Lighting: The Dudley Project', in R.V. Clarke (ed.), *Situational Crime Prevention – Successful Case Studies* (2nd edition), Harrow & Heston, Guilderland, New York.

Palmer, E.J., A. Holmes and C.R. Hollin, 2002. 'Investigating Burglars' Decisions: Factors Influencing Target Choice, Method of Entry, Reasons for Offending, Repeat Victimisation of a Property and Victim Awareness' *Security Journal*, 15(1): 7–18

Pascoe, T., 1991. *The BRE Watford Burglary Study, Part 2 – Domestic Premises*, N20/91, Building Research Establishment, Garston, Watford.

Pascoe, T., 1993. *Domestic burglaries: the police view*, BRE Information Paper IP 20/93, Building Research Establishment, Garston, Watford.

Pease, K., 1999. *Lighting and Crime*, Institution of Lighting Engineers, Rugby, Warwickshire.

Poyner, B., 1983. *Design against Crime*, Butterworths, London.

Poyner, B. and B. Webb, 1991. *Crime Free Housing*, Butterworth Architecture, Oxford.

Poyner, B., P. Helson and B. Webb, 1985. *Layout of Residential Areas and Its Influence on Crime*, Tavistock Institute of Human Relations (2T 508), London.

Rengert, G. and S. Hakin, (1998). 'Burglary in Affluent Communities: A Planning Perspective', in Felson, M. and R.B. Peiser (eds), *Reducing Crime – Through Real Estate Development and Management*. Urban Land Institute, Washington, DC. pp. 39–52.

Sallybanks, J. and N. Thomas, 2000. 'Thefts of External Vehicle Parts: An Emerging Problem' *Crime Prevention and Community Safety: An International Journal*, 2(3): 17–22.

Schneider, R.H. and T. Kitchen, 2002. *Planning for Crime Prevention: A Transatlantic Perspective*, Routledge, London.

Shaw, K.T. and R. Gifford, 1994. 'Residents' and Burglars' Assessment of Burglary Risk from Defensible Space Cues', *Journal of Environmental Pychology*, 14(3): 177–94.

Sheard, M., 1991. *Report on Burglary Patterns: The Impact of Cul-de-sacs*, Delta Police Department, British Columbia. (An unpublished report quoted in Beavon Brantingham and Brantingham, 1994.)

Simmonds, J. and colleagues, 2002. *Crime in England and Wales 2001/2002*, Home Office, London. See publications.rds@homeoffice.gsi.gov.uk.

Southall, D. and P. Ekblom, 1985. *Designing for Vehicle Security: Towards a Crime Free Car*, Crime Prevention Unit Paper 4, Home Office, London.

Stollard, P. (ed.), 1991. *Crime Prevention through Housing Design*, Spon, London.

Topping, P. and T. Pascoe, 2000. 'Countering Household Burglary through the Secured by Design Scheme: Does it Work? An Assessment of the Evidence, 1989–1999', *Security Journal*, 13(4): 71–8.

Urban Task Force, 1999, *Towards an Urban Renaissance*, Spon, London.

Ward, C. (ed.), 1973. *Vandalism*, Architectural Press, London.

Warren, F. and P. Stollard, 1988. *Safe as Houses – a review of the importance of housing design and layout in achieving security*, Institute of Advanced Architectural Studies, University of York.

Wilson, S., 1980. 'Vandalism and "Defensible Space" on London Housing Estates', in R.V.G. Clarke and P. Mayhew (eds), *Designing Out Crime*, Home Office Research Unit, HMSO, London.

Winchester, S. and H. Jackson, 1982. *Residential Burglary: The Limits of Prevention*, Home Office Research Study No. 74, HMSO, London.

Index

Added to the page references, 'f' denotes a figure, 'n' denotes a footnote and 't' denotes a table.